United States
Department of
Agriculture

Forest Service

Pacific Northwest
Research Station

General Technical
Report
PNW-GTR-748
April 2008

User Guide for HCR Estimator 2.0: Software to Calculate Cost and Revenue Thresholds for Harvesting Small-Diameter Ponderosa Pine

Dennis R. Becker, Debra Larson,
Eini C. Lowell, and Robert B. Rummer

Authors

Dennis R. Becker is an assistant professor, University of Minnesota, Department of Forest Resources, 1530 Cleveland Ave. N, St. Paul, MN 55108-6112; **Debra Larson** is a professor, Northern Arizona University, College of Engineering and Natural Sciences, Flagstaff, AZ 86011; **Eini C. Lowell** is a research forest products technologist, U.S. Department of Agriculture, Forest Service, Pacific Northwest Research Station, 620 SW Main, Suite 400, Portland, OR 97205; **Robert B. Rummer** is a research engineer, U.S. Department of Agriculture, Forest Service, Southern Research Station, Forest Operations and Engineering Research Unit, 520 Devall Drive, Auburn, AL 36830.

Abstract

Becker, Dennis R.; Larson, Debra; Lowell, Eini C.; Rummer, Robert B. 2007.
User guide for HCR Estimator 2.0: software to calculate cost and revenue
thresholds for harvesting small-diameter ponderosa pine. Gen. Tech. Rep.
PNW-GTR-748. Portland, OR: U.S. Department of Agriculture, Forest Service,
Pacific Northwest Research Station. 51 p.

The HCR (Harvest Cost-Revenue) Estimator is engineering and financial analysis
software used to evaluate stand-level financial thresholds for harvesting small-
diameter ponderosa pine (*Pinus ponderosa* Dougl. ex Laws.) in the Southwest
United States. The Windows-based program helps contractors and planners to
identify costs associated with tree selection, residual handling, transportation of
raw materials, and equipment used. Costs are compared against total financial
return for regionally based market opportunities to arrive at potential net profit.
Information is used to identify per-acre cost thresholds, for contract appraisal, and
for prioritizing project planning for wildfire fuel reduction treatments and forest
restoration efforts.

Keywords: Financial analysis software, simulation, harvest costs, market
values, small-diameter ponderosa pine utilization (Southwest).

Contents

Introduction

Fuel reduction treatments generate a large amount of woody biomass, most of which is small in diameter and of marginal economic value. Opportunities to process this material are few in the Southwestern United States (Keegan et al. 2001a, 2001b; Spelter and Alderman 2005), limiting the ability to reduce the threat of wildfire to communities. Compounding the problem are estimates of harvest and transport costs for biomass that are either incomplete or based on localized knowledge not applicable to other areas. There is inconsistent knowledge of the critical cost factors, lending to discrepancies in contract bid rates and the financial viability of wood products businesses—the viability of which is necessary to aid in reducing the risk of catastrophic wildfire on public and private lands. Better estimates of harvest costs and product values, including better calculations of merchantable volumes, will expedite implementation of fuel reduction projects.

Application of the Harvest Cost-Revenue Estimator

This manual reports on the usage of a Windows-based, public domain financial and engineering software program called the Harvest Cost-Revenue (HCR) Estimator. The software is used to evaluate stand-level financial cost and revenue thresholds for harvesting small-diameter ponderosa pine (*Pinus ponderosa* Dougl. ex Laws.) in the Southwest United States. The HCR Estimator is based on an accumulation of scientific and engineering information on harvest costs and product values necessary for identifying financial thresholds of fuel reduction projects. The software was developed for use by logging contractors and forest planners to lower their costs of fuel reduction treatments through evaluation of in-woods decisionmaking regarding tree selection, residuals left on site, and product suitability for regionally based markets. Because different markets require logs of various sizes and quality, it is important that forest planners and contractors be able to estimate project costs for varying harvest specifications and transportation distances. These costs, along with possible offsets from stewardship and service contracts, are compared against total financial return to arrive at potential net profit. This information can then be used to identify per-acre cost thresholds, appraise contract bid rates, prioritize fuel reduction treatments, and assess stumpage values for small-diameter timber and biomass. It also is useful in assessing the feasibility of prospective small-wood utilization enterprises for heating and electricity, wood-plastic composites, bio-chemicals, engineered lumber, and other value-added products.

The HCR Estimator represents the next generation of fuel reduction modeling of treatment costs and financial returns given available biomass and solid-wood markets (Fight and Barbour 2005, Larson and Mirth 2004). It provides a critical step in the development of a fully integrated system from silvicultural prescription through stem selection, harvesting, processing, transport, and market selection. At every functional step, a decision is made about the possible allocation of woody material either to further processing or to being left in the woods. In an integrated system, each decision is informed by knowledge about the capabilities of subsequent functions. Together, they provide information on the financial viability of fuel treatment programs. The appeal of a financial analysis program like the HCR Estimator is that costs can be estimated for uniquely tailored harvest systems and stand prescriptions, and compared against revenue for regionally based biomass and log market opportunities. The software is further tailored to reflect the volume and taper of ponderosa pine trees in the Southwest, which affects product recovery and, to a lesser extent, equipment productivity.

Development of the HCR Estimator was supported by funding from the Joint Fire Science Program of the National Fire Plan. Researchers at the Pacific Northwest Research Station, Southern Research Station, Northern Arizona University, and the University of Minnesota created the program with assistance from the Rocky Mountain Research Station, Greater Flagstaff Forests Partnership, Southwest Sustainable Forests Partnership, Northern Arizona Wood Products Association, and the Colorado Wood Utilization and Marketing Program.

Model Users

The target audience for the HCR Estimator includes forest planners, contractors and loggers, consultants, and community development and nonprofit organizations. The model allows forest planners to conduct project appraisal, evaluate contract bid rates, and assess the stumpage value of material removed. Contractors are able to use the model to estimate operation and maintenance costs of equipment and generate detailed cost-revenue estimates for project bidding. The model can be further used to assess project feasibility, assist in project design, and for community development purposes for business expansion and development. The HCR Estimator is not intended to take the place of sound financial analysis, but to supplement business planning.

Software Disclaimer

The HCR Estimator software is in the public domain. The recipient may neither assert propriety rights thereto nor represent them to anyone as other than government-produced programs. The use of trade or firm names in this publication and in the software is for the information of the reader. Such use does not constitute an official endorsement by the U.S. Department of Agriculture of any product or service to the exclusion of others that may be suitable.

The software was developed for ponderosa pine in the Southwest United States. Application for other tree species is not valid. In other regions of the country, ponderosa pine may be subject to different growing conditions, which may influence equipment productivity and volume recovery of solid wood and biomass material from individual trees.

It is important to remember that the HCR Estimator is a decision-support tool to assist users in making choices regarding in-woods tree selection, equipment optimization, and market selection. Because it is not possible to include the full range of harvesting options and market scenarios available, users must exercise discretion when comparing outputs and evaluating project costs. The HCR Estimator is not to be used in lieu of sound business planning and a thorough financial analysis. The accuracy of the software relies on the quality of data entered and the degree to which it reflects situations on the ground. "Estimating is not an exact science. Experience, judgment, and care should enable an estimator to prepare an estimate that will reasonably approximate the ultimate costs of the project" (Peurifoy and Oberlender 2002).

Getting Started

User Inputs

Default inputs are available for nonspecific financial simulations. Where more accurate cost-revenue estimates are required, the following information is necessary:

- Cut-tree list from a timber cruise of the desired project area.
- Identified harvest operations including number and size of machines used, labor costs, operating conditions, and annual utilization rates.
- Contract details including acreage, stumpage or service rates, and treatment techniques for slash and residual trees too small for biomass or log markets.
- Raw material market specifications including intended outlet(s), size specifications, moisture content, and distance to market(s).

The HCR Estimator relies on an internal log calculator to determine merchantable volumes and log potential as a function of stand data and market conditions. Merchantable tree definitions and log volumes are calculated directly from tree data and log market specifications. Follow-on predictions of treatment activities are linked directly to log potential, better reflecting true stand conditions, harvest costs, and ultimately revenue potential. The model has three parts:

Log Calculator—Calculates log size, number, and volume (cubic feet, tons) from harvest prescriptions as a function of cut trees and market specifications.

Cost Estimator—Determines harvesting and transportation costs from production rate relationships, equipment and labor costs, trucking information, and cut-tree and log data.

Revenue Predictor—Estimates net financial return for the biomass and logs removed from forest treatments and sold to primary and secondary manufacturing businesses. Financial returns are based on existing market specifications in the region. For instance, logs with a 4-in small-end diameter (SED) (inside bark) that are 16 ft long and used to make wood pallets will have a different market value than logs having a 6-in SED that are 24-ft in length and used for dimension lumber.

The HCR Estimator calculates financial return by determining which trees will generate logs that meet user-defined markets. If, for instance, the greatest return is from logs used for dimension lumber, the model will allocate the maximum number of logs that meet market specifications for that end use based on the specified size of logs. Remaining logs and biomass from smaller trees are then allocated according to the next highest raw material market value as a function of log size. Different markets will presumably have different costs of harvesting, handling, and transport. Aggregated costs are compared against gross financial return to arrive at potential net profit. Table 1 displays user-defined inputs in relation to software outputs.

Software Outputs

The HCR Estimator provides various outputs to facilitate user needs. Among those are the size, number, and volume of logs, volume of biomass, project harvest costs, labor costs, equipment mobilization, and handling and transportation costs. Gross revenue is generated by market type, which allows for comparison of market opportunities and simulation. The required inputs and model outputs are shown in table 1.

Installing the HCR Estimator Software

The HCR Estimator has been programmed using Visual Basic® software, allowing for use on most Windows-based operating systems. System requirements include 12 MB of hard-drive space and the most current Microsoft®.NET framework. To install the latest version of the software, download the program from the following Web site and follow the instructions in the installation wizard displayed in figures 1(a) and 1(b): http://www.fs.fed.us/pnw/publications/gtr748. All files necessary to run the application will be automatically downloaded on the hard disk and a

Table 1—User inputs and Harvest Cost-Revenue (HCR) Estimator model outputs

User-defined inputs	HCR Estimator outputs
Per-acre cut-tree data (by size class)	Log size, number, and volume
Harvesting system (equipment used)	Volume of clean/dirty chips generated
Equipment age, price, horsepower, years owned, annual usage	Project costs as a function of labor and equipment costs (ownership, operation, and maintenance)
Employee wage rates and benefits	Stumpage costs or service contract
Equipment mobilization distance	Mobilization costs
Simulated log and biomass market(s)	Truckloads by market, transport costs
Market specifications, distance	Gross revenue by market
Overhead and indirect costs	Net revenue (loss) potential of project
Desired profit margin	

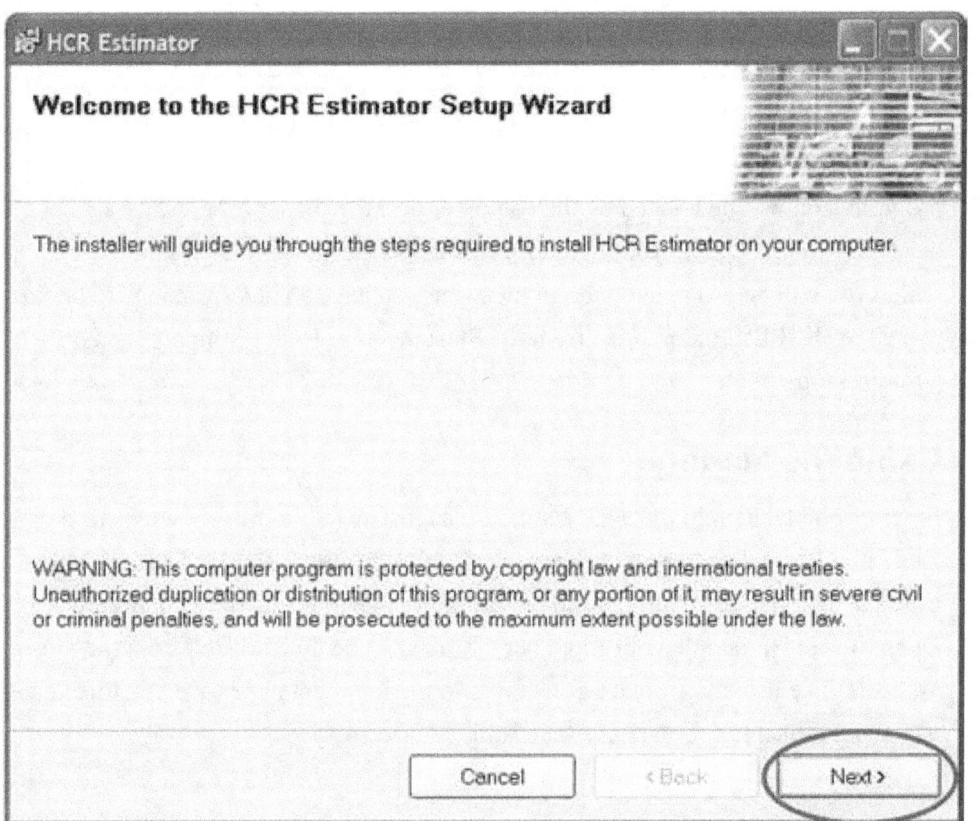

Figure 1a—HCR Estimator install computer screens: (a) opening screen and (b) installation specifics.

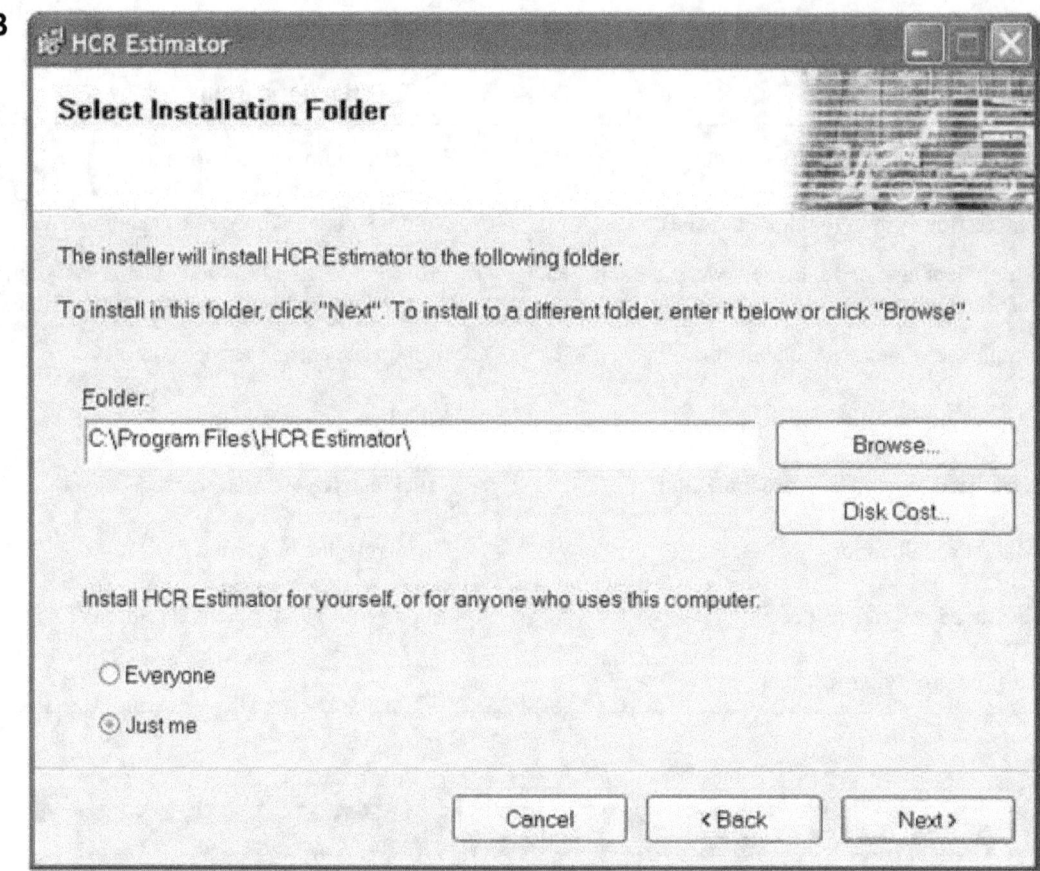

Figure 1b—HCR Estimator install computer screens: (a) opening screen and (b) installation specifics.

program icon will be created on the computer desktop. In some cases, it may be necessary to first update your operating system to the latest .NET framework, which you will be prompted to do in the event you have an older version. To begin using the HCR Estimator, open from the Start menu or HCR Estimator icon on your desktop.

Using the Model

Enter original data into the HCR Estimator as instructed in the following steps or load preexisting data to provide an example of user inputs. To load the companion example data file, select "Load Model" from the File menu as shown in figure 2. Open the file, "Example User Input.hcr," which can be downloaded from the project Web site. The user may make any changes to the input data and save as a different name and return to this data at a later time.

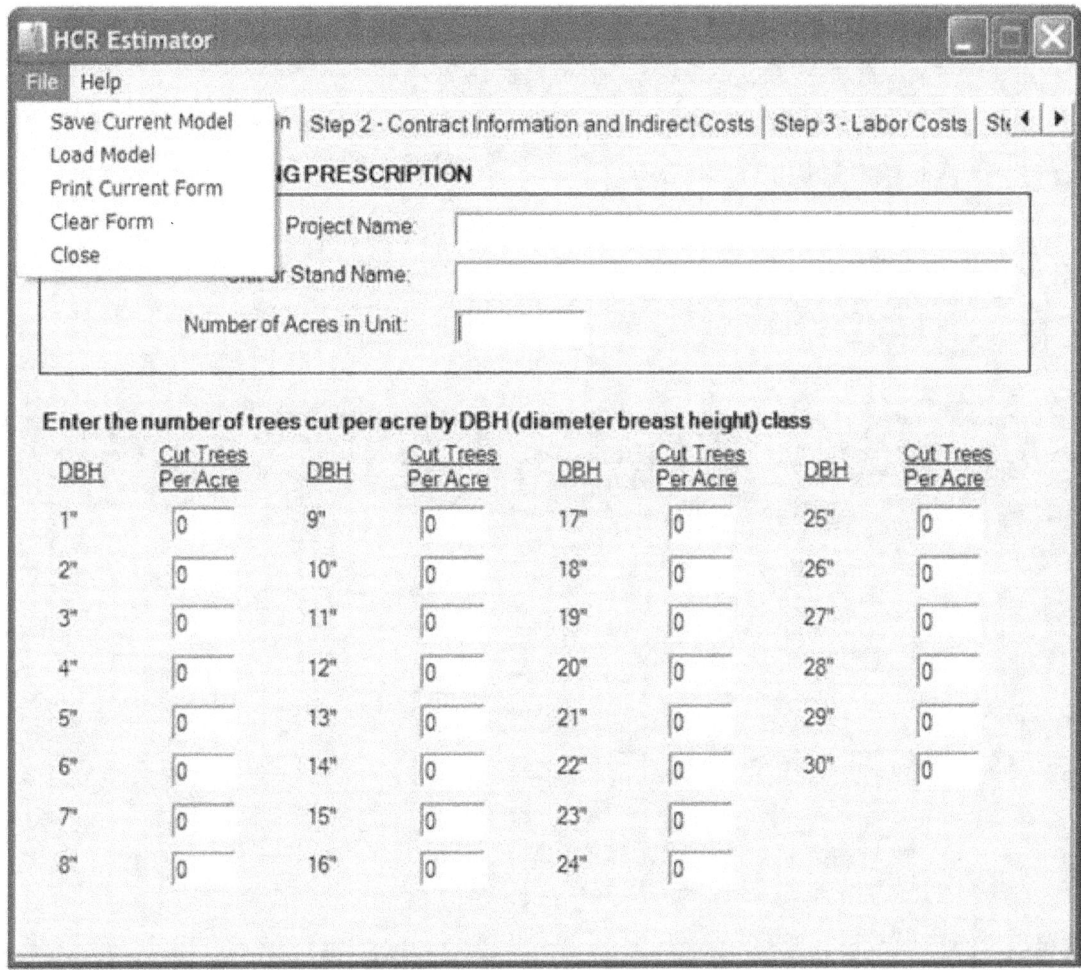

Figure 2—HCR Estimator step 1 cutting prescription screen to enter project details and cut tree information.

Step 1—Cutting Prescription

In this step, users provide the cut-tree data, also referred to as the cutting prescription, for the project area they wish to assess. Enter the following information on the screen shown in figure 3.

Project name—
Enter the project name in the box. This information is optional but provides a way to identify different project simulations and track results.

Unit or stand name—
Enter the unit or stand name in the corresponding box. This information is optional but also provides a way to identify different project simulations or to compare costs and revenue for different stands or prescriptions within the same area.

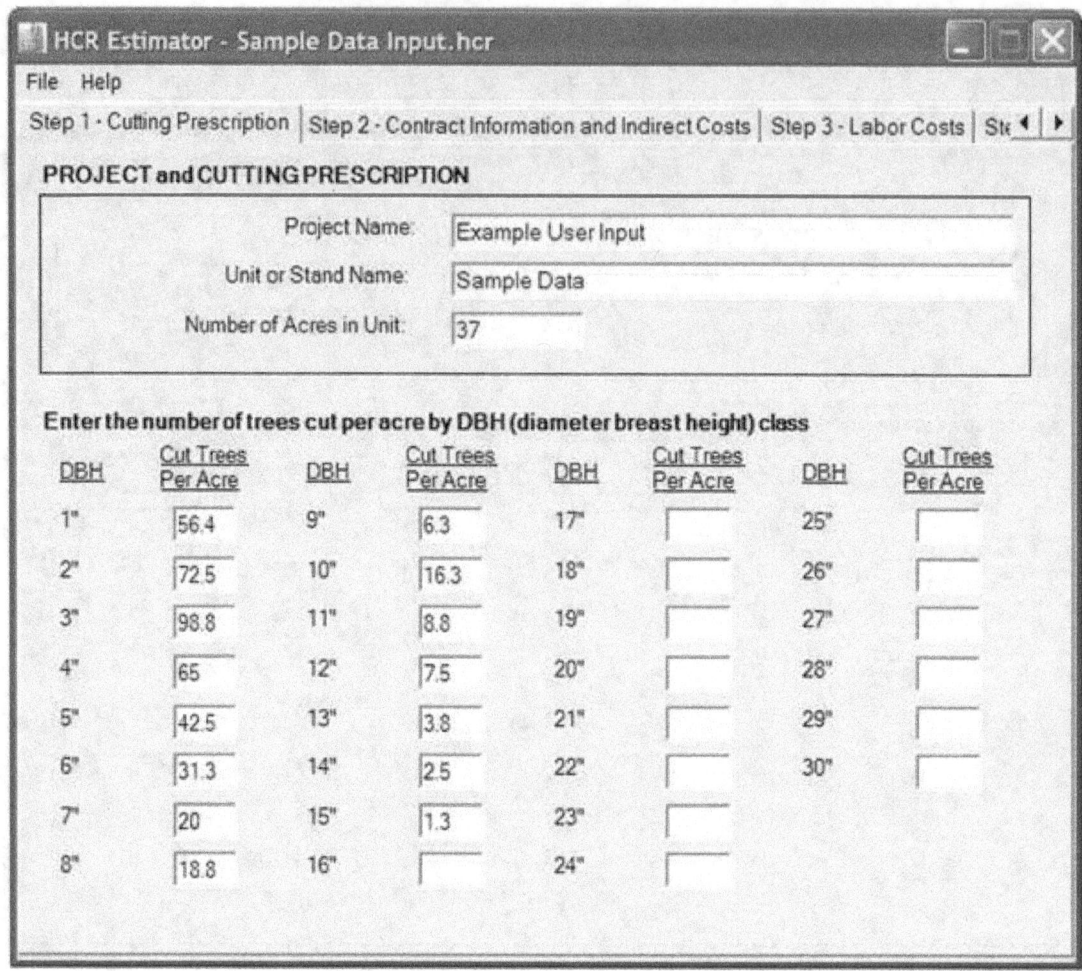

Figure 3—HCR Estimator step 1 cutting prescription screen with data.

Number of acres in unit—
Enter the total number of acres to be assessed for a particular harvest unit or forest stand. Project costs and net revenues are calculated as a function of total acres. Enter only numeric characters (e.g., 37, 123.4). Spaces and symbols may not be used.

Number of trees cut per acre—
Enter the anticipated average number of trees to be cut per acre by tree diameter at breast height (DBH). If there are no trees to be cut in a specific diameter class, enter "0" in the corresponding box or leave blank.

The number of cut trees per acre can be obtained from timber cruise data. These data are routinely provided in sale notification documents if working with federal or state agencies or can be requested of the landowner. If the number of trees cut per acre is unknown for 1-in diameter classes, users may enter cut tree estimates by 2-in diameter classes in either the even or odd-numbered diameter boxes. Enter a "0" or leave blank the intervening classes. For instance, if from the cruise data it is known that 12 trees will be cut in the 6- to 8-in diameter class, users may enter 12 in the box for either 6 or 7 in. Alternately, they could enter six trees in each of the two classes.

Step 2—Contract Information and Indirect Costs

In this section (fig. 4), users provide contract information and items that contribute indirectly to harvesting costs. For example, service contract bid rate, stumpage rate, and road work allotment are entered here, if applicable. Indirect harvesting costs include expected profit, administrative overhead, and other indirect operations costs.

Service contract bid ($/acre)—
This is the amount paid by the landowner, per acre, to the contractor for work performed. Where the service contract amount is unknown, users can leave it blank to

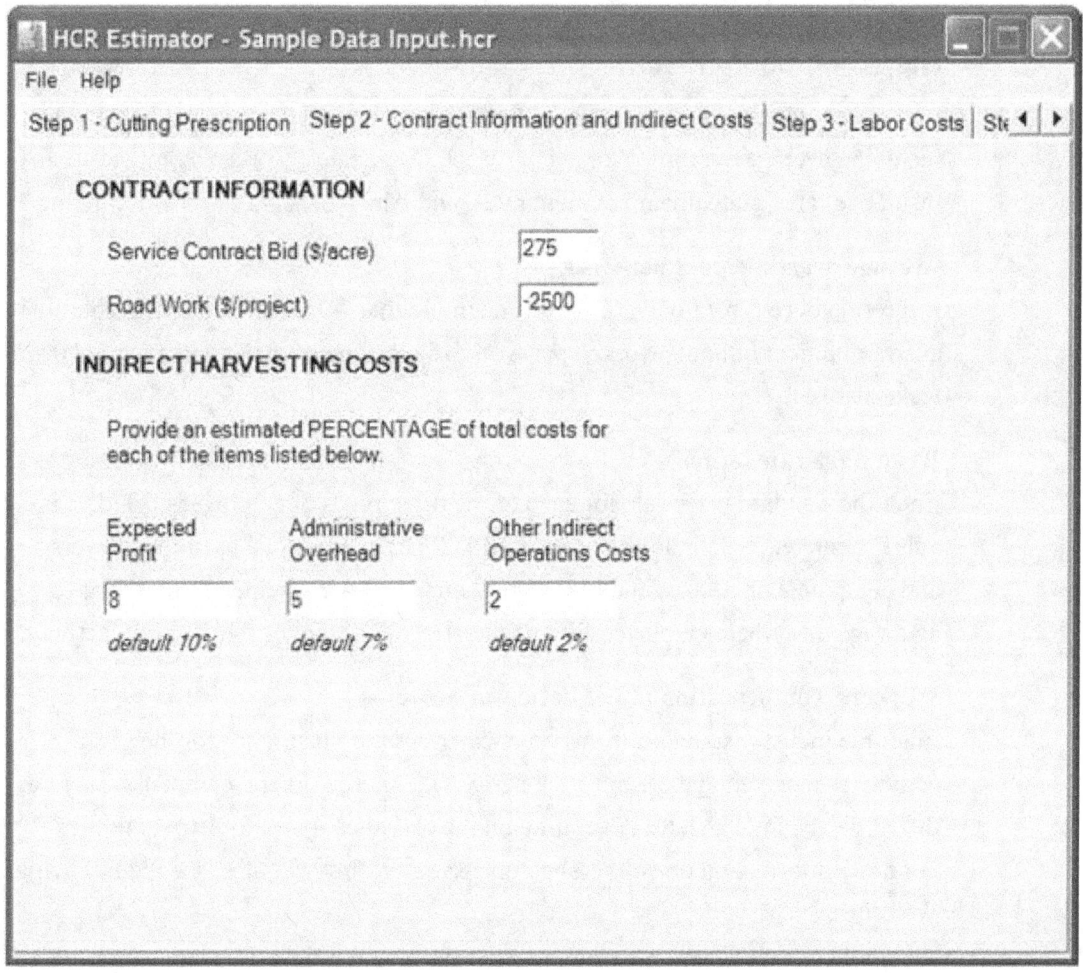

Figure 4—HCR Estimator step 2 contract information and indirect cost screen.

assess financial shortfalls in economic return or enter a desired service contract bid rate to assess different scenarios. Enter the amount of the service contract per acre.

Road work ($/project)—

This is the amount of money paid by the landowner to the contractor to build roads or make road improvements, or by the contractor for road maintenance and repairs. Where costs are incurred, enter as a negative value (e.g., -$2,500). Enter the lump sum amount, if applicable, paid for road work.

Indirect harvesting costs—

For each of the three indirect costs shown in figure 4, enter the estimated or desired percentage of total cost of the project. If any of the boxes are left blank, the indicated default value will be used. Administrative overhead includes a woods boss, maintenance shop mechanic, office staff, buildings, and fuel trucks. Other indirect costs include operations not covered elsewhere, for example, the use of water tenders for road dust abatement or costs for grass seeding.

Step 3—Labor Costs

In this step, users provide descriptive information about labor costs for employees, including average overtime worked per week, wage rates, workers compensation insurance rates, state unemployment rates, and fringe benefits as shown in figure 5.

Average overtime paid per week—

If the employee typically works overtime (more than 40 hours per week), enter the average number of hours worked per week. If overtime does not occur, enter "0" or leave blank.

Basic wage rate ($/hr)—

Enter the standard wage rate for each of the three types of employees listed. If no value is entered, a default wage rate of $19.00 per hour will be used for sawyers and equipment operators, and $13.00 per hour for general helpers. Enter the average wage rate where employees are paid different wage rates for the same activity.

Workers' compensation (% of basic wage rate)—

Enter the industry standard for workers compensation insurance for the given activity as a percentage of employee basic wage rate. Workers' compensation rates differ widely among states depending on the classification of forestry activities. For more information on workers' compensation insurance rates, see the following Web sites:
- State workers' compensation division (http://www.dol.gov/esa/regs/compliance/owcp/wc.htm)

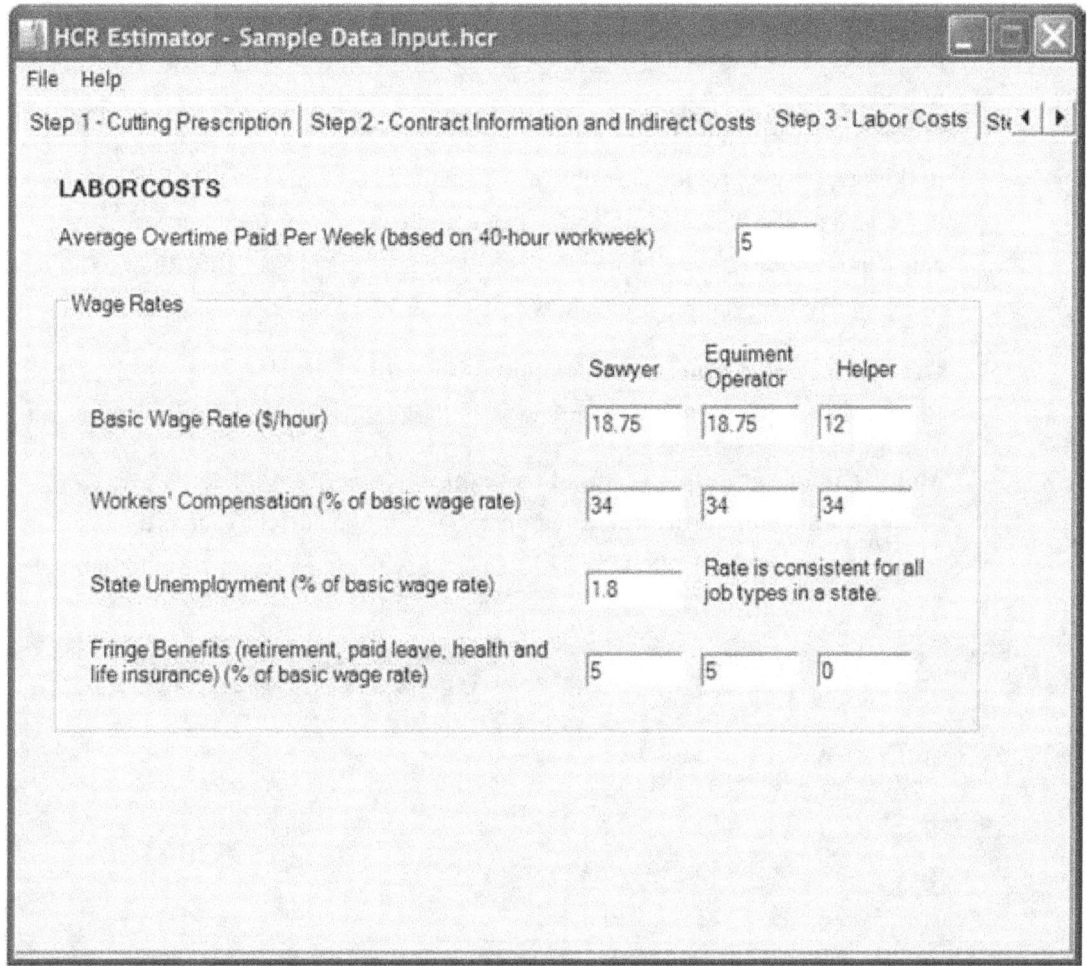

Figure 5—HCR Estimator step 3 labor costs input screen.

- National Council on Compensation Insurance, Scopes Manual Classification (https://www.ncci.com)

State unemployment (% of basic wage rate)—
Enter the state unemployment insurance rate as a percentage of the basic wage rate. Unemployment rates are consistent for all employees within a state for any type of work performed. For more information on state rates see the following Web site:
- State employment office (http://workforcesecurity.doleta.gov/map.asp)

Fringe benefits (% of basic wage rate)—
Employers may contribute to retirement plans, provide paid time off or leave, or provide health and life insurance for employees. Enter the fringe benefit rate as a percentage of the basic rate. If benefits are not provided, the corresponding boxes

may be left blank. Note that fringe benefits do not include legally required benefits for social security, Medicare, unemployment, and workers compensation.

Step 4—Equipment

In this step, users provide descriptive information about the type(s) of equipment to be used to complete the project, which equipment will be used to process wood chips and residuals, and the operating conditions of the project site. Refer to figures 6, 7a, and 7b for example user inputs.

Off-highway diesel fuel cost ($/gallon)—
Enter the price per gallon of off-highway-grade fuel used in harvesting equipment.

Months of operation/harvesting this year—
Enter the total months of anticipated operations for the current year as a whole number or decimal (e.g., 9, 9.75). This is used to calculate project costs for annual

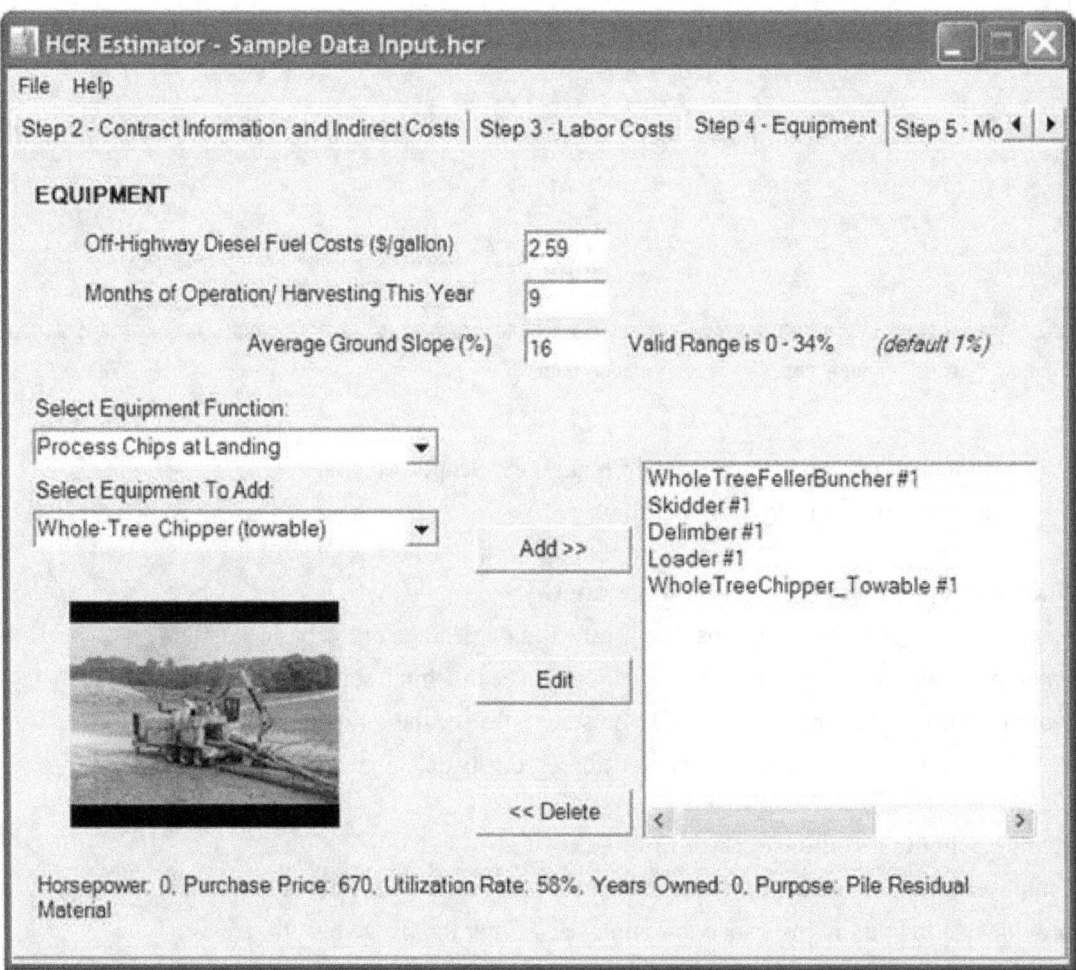

Figure 6—HCR Estimator step 4 equipment input screen.

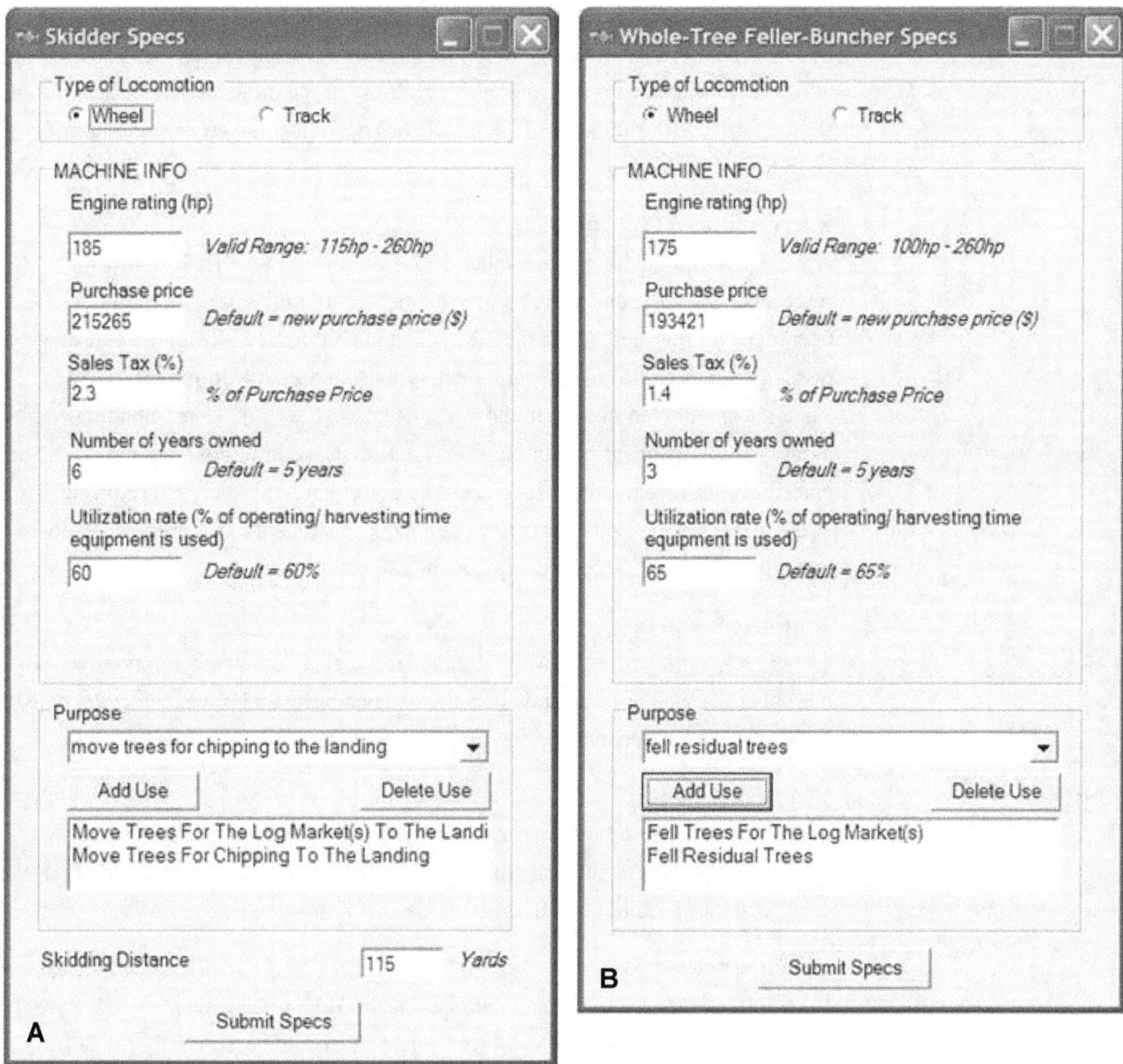

Figure 7—Examples of underlying screens (step 4) for equipment specifications.

equipment operation and ownership. For instance, it may be feasible to harvest trees year-round; thus loan payments and depreciation costs can be spread out over a greater number of acres. Where fewer acres are harvested because of seasonal closures for rain, snow, or wildfire, per-acre costs may increase.

Average ground slope (%)—
Enter the average ground slope for the unit assessed. Where slope varies considerably over the harvest unit, users should consider separating into smaller units with

uniform slope conditions. Equipment productivity rates used in the HCR Estimator are valid on slopes ranging from 0 to 34 percent. A default value of 1 percent will be used if a value is not entered. Operability of the project site is based on a standard harvesting situation. The model does not adjust for severe conditions or extraordinary circumstances.

Select equipment function—
A variety of equipment sets are valid. Those simulated in the HCR Estimator represent harvesting and processing equipment commonly used for commercial operations. In this step, select the desired equipment function from the pull-down menu. Next select the desired equipment type from **Select Equipment To Add**. Then select "Add" to include in the dialogue box to the right. Corresponding equipment forms will appear prompting user inputs displayed in figures 7a and 7b. After entering required equipment specifications, select "Submit Specs" to return to step 4. Users can select "Edit" to change equipment specifications. To remove equipment, highlight that piece of equipment and select "Delete."

Type of locomotion—
The cut-to-length harvester, whole-tree feller-buncher, skidder, and forwarder will be rubber wheeled or tracked, which affects operability and price. Select the type of locomotion for corresponding equipment selected in step 4, if applicable.

Engine rating (hp)—
Enter the total engine horsepower rating (hp) as provided by the manufacturer. Horsepower is used to calculate maintenance and operation costs including fuel usage and the speed of operation.

Purchase price—
Enter the new or used equipment purchase price. If no price is given or is unknown, a default new purchase price will be calculated based on horsepower ratings and equipment values by region of the country. Equipment depreciation is calculated by using the new or used equipment price as entered.

Sales tax—
Enter applicable sales tax for the purchase price of the equipment.

Number of years owned—
Enter the total number of years the equipment has been owned by the current owner. The number of years owned, which is different than the total age of the equipment, is used to calculate the remaining loan period on an assumed

amortization period of 5 years. Equipment owned for 5 or more years is assumed paid off regardless of purchase price.

Utilization rate—
Enter the percentage of total operating time equipment is used for its intended purpose. To calculate the utilization rate, first determine the total number of hours of anticipated operations per year from the entry in step 4, **Months of Operation/Harvesting This Year**. Assuming 10 months of operations per year with an average of 4.5 weeks per month and 40 hours work per week, total "scheduled machine hours" is 1,800. Next calculate total "productive machine hours" the piece of equipment is being used for its stated purpose. Assuming time spent for daily equipment maintenance, refueling, and rest breaks, equipment could be in operation a total of 1,080 hours or 60 percent. Enter 60 in the box for the "utilization rate." Default values are provided for all equipment regardless of type.

Purpose—
Select the intended use(s) of each piece of equipment from the pull-down menu and select "Add Use." Users must repeat this step for each desired equipment purpose. To remove, highlight the task and select "Delete Use." When all intended uses have been defined, select "Submit Specs" for the software to calculate costs.

Additional user inputs may be required for specific types of equipment. One-way **Skidding Distance** or **Forwarding Distance** (yards) is required for moving trees and logs to a landing for processing. **Bunk size** (cubic feet) is necessary for the forwarder to determine load capacity. Also, if harvesting with chainsaws, subcontractors (hand fellers) may be selected.

Step 5—Mobilization

In this step, users provide information specific to the mobilization of equipment to the project site, specifically the number of miles and travel speed as shown in figure 8.

Distance and time to move equipment to site—
Enter the number of miles (one-way) to move machinery in the first box. In the second box enter the average speed (mph) traveled to the site with the equipment, and in the third box enter the average return speed without equipment (mph).

Mobilization equipment—
This section refers to the semi truck and trailer used to transport equipment to the project site. Enter the purchase price and number of years owned by the current

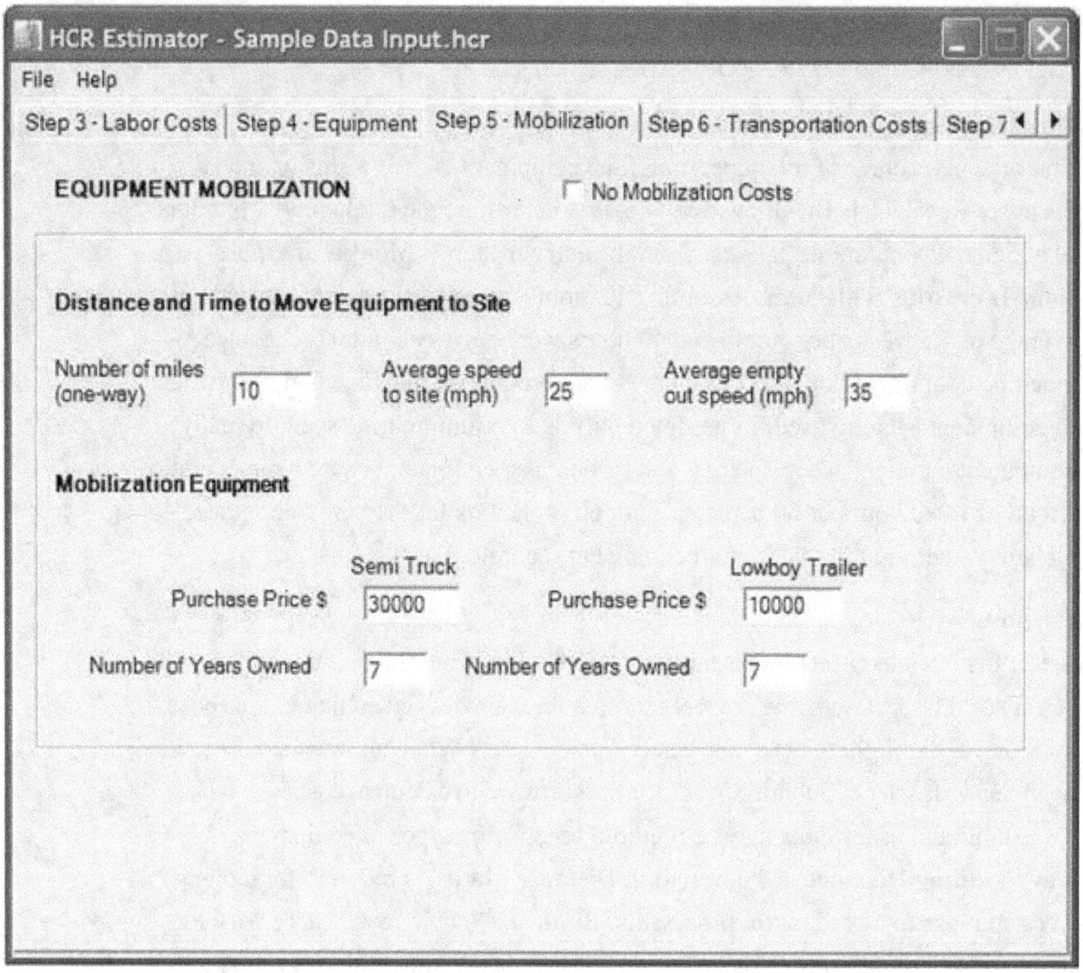

Figure 8—HCR Estimator step 5 equipment mobilization input screen.

owner for both the semi truck and an equipment trailer. The default purchase prices for the semi and trailer are $50,000 and $10,000 respectively, with an assumed 5 years of ownership. If no mobilization of equipment is necessary because of proximity to previous project site or because a third party is responsible for transporting the equipment, the "No Mobilization Costs" box can be selected.

Step 6—Transportation Costs

In this step, users provide information about transportation costs including trucking rates, load and drop times, and log and chip van weights shown in figure 9. This information is used to calculate transportation costs associated with different market scenarios.

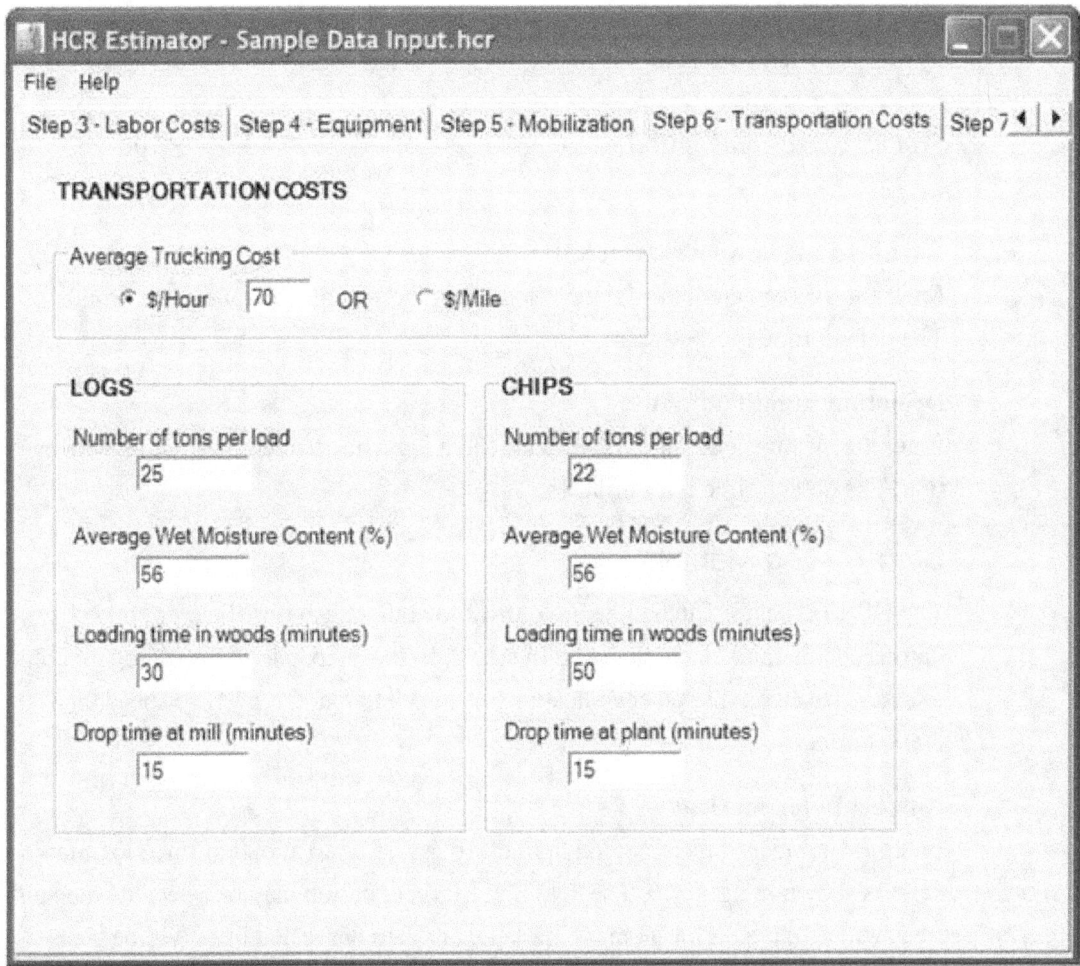

Figure 9—HCR Estimator step 6 transportation costs input screen.

Average trucking cost—
Select either $/hour or $/mile depending on the trucking cost basis used. The default value is $65 per hour. In either case, fuel costs are incorporated into the trucking cost estimate.

Number of tons per load—
Enter the average tons per load for both logging trucks and chip vans so that the total number of truckloads can be calculated for the respective markets chosen in step 8. The default value is 25 tons for logs and chips. However, legal highway limits may differ because of trailer configuration.

Average wet moisture content (%)—
Enter the **wet** moisture content of the logs and chips at the time of shipping so that

the total number of truckloads can be calculated. Wet moisture content is calculated by the following equation:

$$Wet\ moisture\ content\ (\%) = \frac{Green\ weight - Oven\text{-}dry\ weight}{Green\ weight} \times 100$$

Loading time in woods (minutes)—
Enter the average amount of time to load log trucks and chip vans in the woods. The default time is 30 minutes.

Drop time at mill (minutes)—
Enter the average amount of time to unload a log truck and chip van at its destination. The default time is 15 minutes.

Step 7—Log Markets

The HCR Estimator can handle up to three log markets at one time, or no log markets. Chip markets are handled in step 8. In this step, users specify log markets to assess based on market specifications, distance to market, average speed, and market price.

Number of log markets—
Enter the number of different log markets to assess up to a total of three log markets, as shown in figure 10. The "No Log Market" option may be selected when all trees will be chipped for biomass markets, or when harvested trees will be transferred from the project site to a log yard but have not yet been sold. For each of the markets selected, corresponding market tabs will appear. Select the corresponding tab to enter market information. Log market specifications described below include small-end diameter, minimum log length, and maximum log length accepted.

Description—
Enter the name of the corresponding market for use in tracking values. For instance, enter "Pallets" for the description of the log market if the first log market is for pallet lumber; enter "Dimension Lumber" if the second market for the next larger logs is for dimension lumber.

Log small-end DIB (inches)—
Enter the smallest log acceptable to log buyers as measured by diameter inside bark at the small end of the log (DIB).

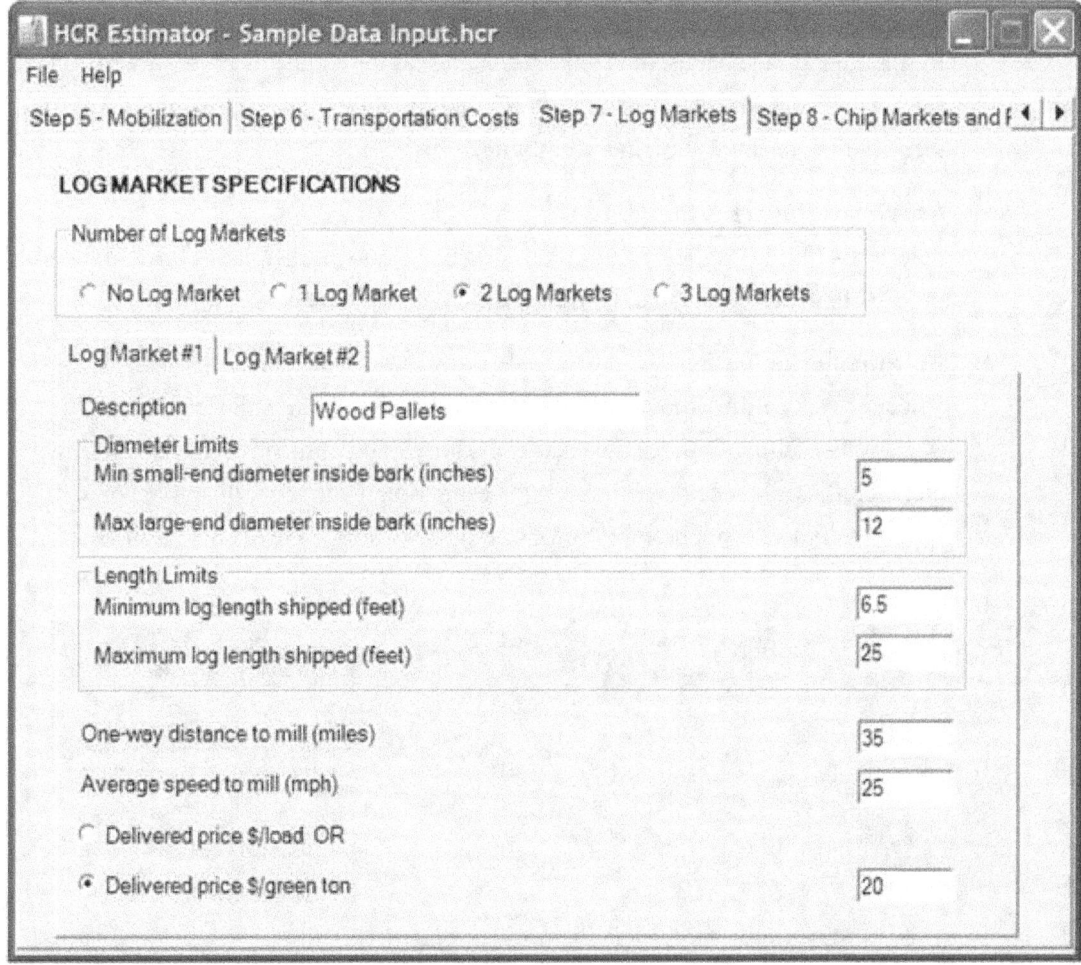

Figure 10—HCR Estimator step 7 available log markets data input screen.

Minimum log length shipped (feet)—

Enter the shortest (end-to-end) log length acceptable to log buyers.

Maximum log length shipped (feet)—

Enter the longest (end-to-end) log length acceptable to log buyers.

One-way distance to mill (miles)—

Enter the total one-way distance to the market destination.

Average speed to mill (mph)—

Enter the average speed to the market destination over all miles traveled to the mill.

Delivered price—

Enter the delivered log price by $/load or $/green ton. Price per green ton is the dollar value of one ton of logs measured by wet moisture content.

Step 8—Chip Markets and Residual

In this step, users specify the commercial market for chips processed from residual slash and trees too small for solid wood markets. If there is no chip market, users identify how residual slash and trees will be disposed of in the woods.

Check box if market for chips—
Select box (fig. 11) if there is a market for chips. If no market, leave box empty and proceed to defining residual handling equipment displayed in figure 12.

No chip market option—
Select among Felling, Mastication, or Do Nothing from the pull-down menu (fig. 11). For felling options, next select the type of equipment from the pull-down menu on the right side of the box. A corresponding equipment dialogue box will appear with user input prompts similar to those in step 4. Select the "Edit" button to

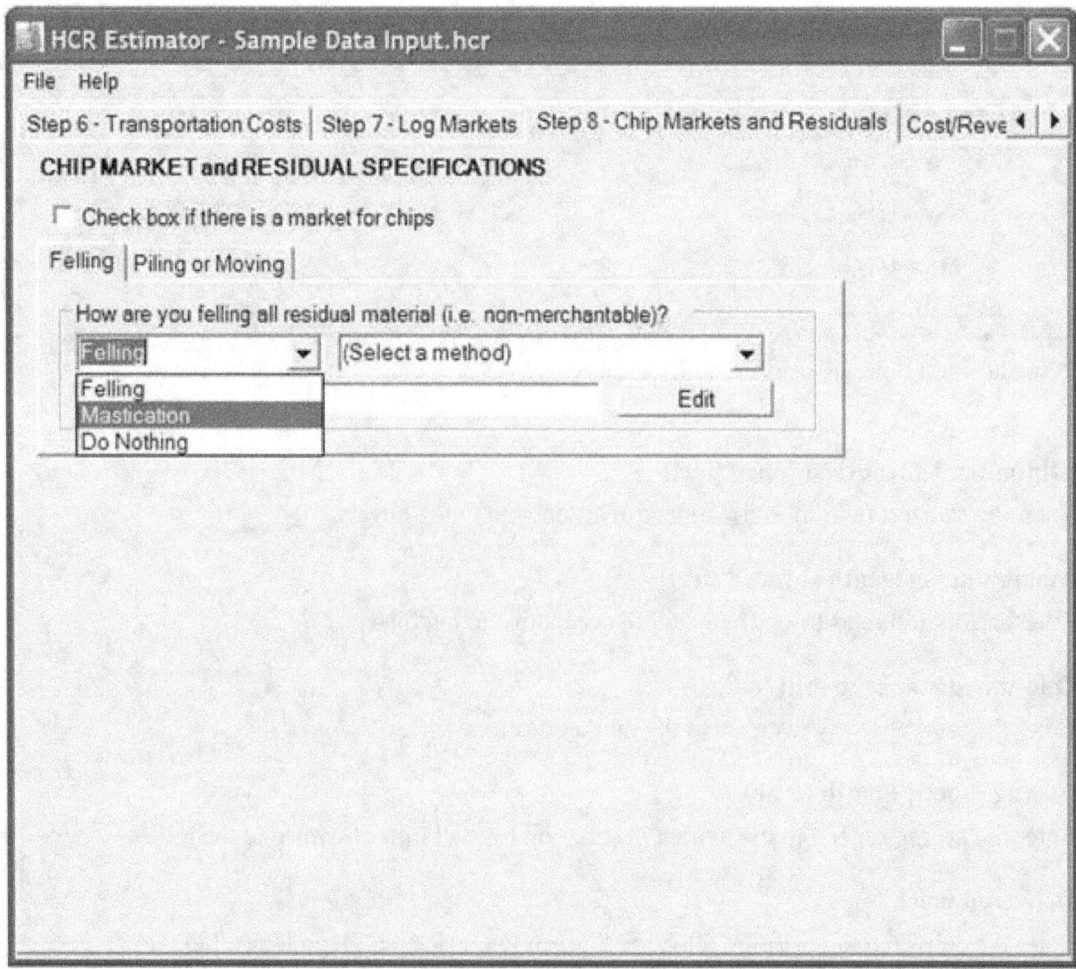

Figure 11—HCR Estimator step 8 identification of available chip market.

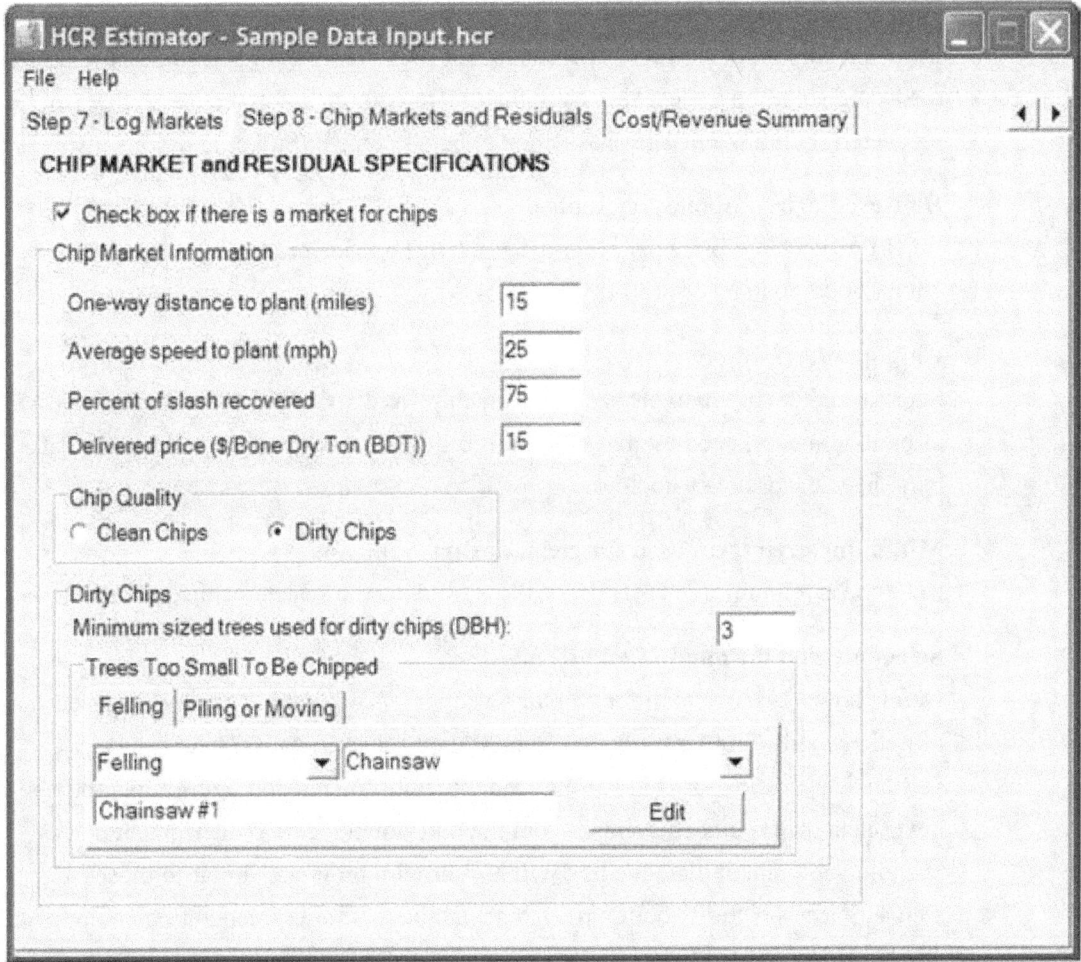

Figure 12—HCR Estimator step 8 data input for chip market and residuals.

change any data inputs for corresponding equipment. To change equipment, select a new type of equipment and enter data input prompts.

Chip market information—
If a commercial chip market exists for either clean or dirty chips, refer to the information below to define transportation costs, slash recovery, delivered price, chip quality and size, and residual slash handling.

One-way distance to plant (miles)—
Enter the total one-way distance to the chip plant.

Average speed to plant (mph)—
Enter the average speed traveled to the chip plant.

Percentage of slash recovered—
Enter the amount of slash, as a percentage of the total slash generated, that will be recovered from the project site. Note that the maximum amount of slash that can be recovered from any one site is assumed to be 84 percent (Stokes and Watson 1991).

Delivered price ($/bone-dry ton)—
Enter the delivered price per bone-dry ton (BDT). Price per BDT is the value of 1 ton (2,000 pounds) of oven-dry biomass.

Chip quality—
Select whether chip markets are for clean chips or dirty chips. Clean chips are free of bark, branches, needles, and other impurities. Dirty chips may include branches, bark, needles, or bole wood.

Minimum sized trees used for clean or dirty chips—
Enter the minimum tree DBH that will be used for the selected chip market.

Select method for handling material—
Define how trees too small for chip or logs markets will be handled or disposed of in the woods. Similar to the No Chip Market scenario above, select among Felling, Mastication, or Do Nothing from the pull-down menu. For felling options, next select the type of equipment from the pull-down menu to the right. A corresponding equipment dialogue box will appear with prompts similar to those in step 4. Select the "Edit" button to change data inputs for corresponding equipment. To change equipment, simply select a new type of equipment and enter the applicable information.

Cost-Revenue Summary

The summary output is organized into a net profit (loss) summary and a biomass utilization summary. The net profit (loss) summary shows costs by type and revenue by market type (figs. 13a and 13b). Scroll to the bottom to see estimated net profit (loss). Per-acre and total project costs and revenue are provided for each equipment function and market scenario to provide users with strategic information for use in optimizing equipment sets, market configurations, and harvest prescriptions.

The Utilization Summary (fig. 13c) is accessed by selecting the green button in the upper right corner. The summary provides a breakdown of the total volume of logs and biomass utilized for selected markets. The total number of logs and truckloads is also calculated for each market to enhance in-woods decisionmaking regarding tree selection and market choice.

A

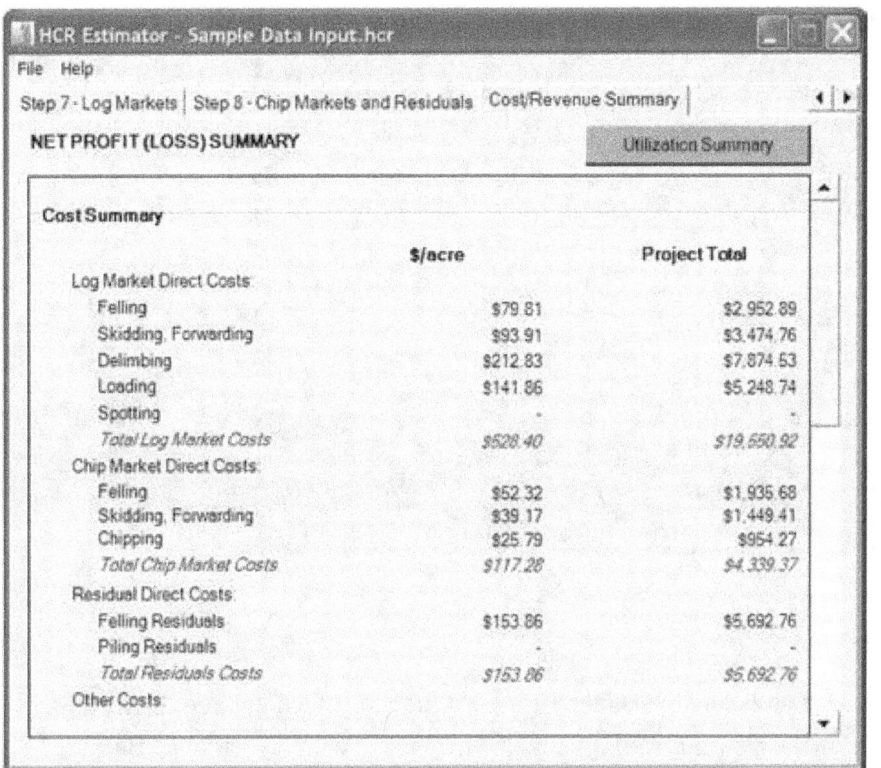

Figure 13—HCR Estimator cost-revenue summaries: (a, b) itemized cost and revenue figures per unit area and for project total and (c) utilization summary for available markets.

B

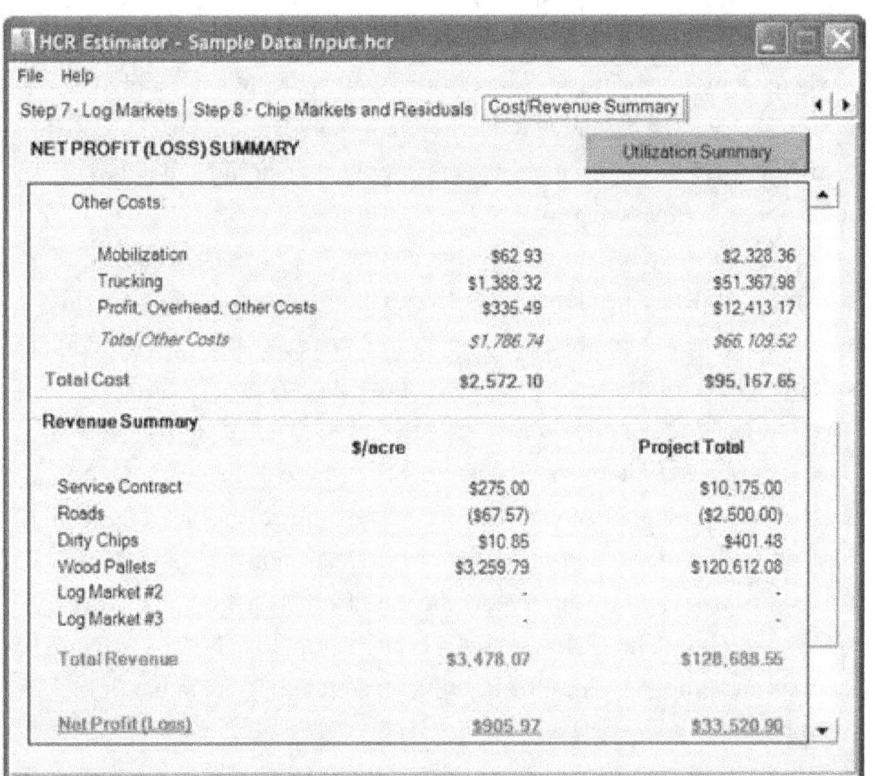

Figure 13—HCR Estimator cost-revenue summaries: (a, b) itemized cost and revenue figures per unit area and for project total and (c) utilization summary for available markets.

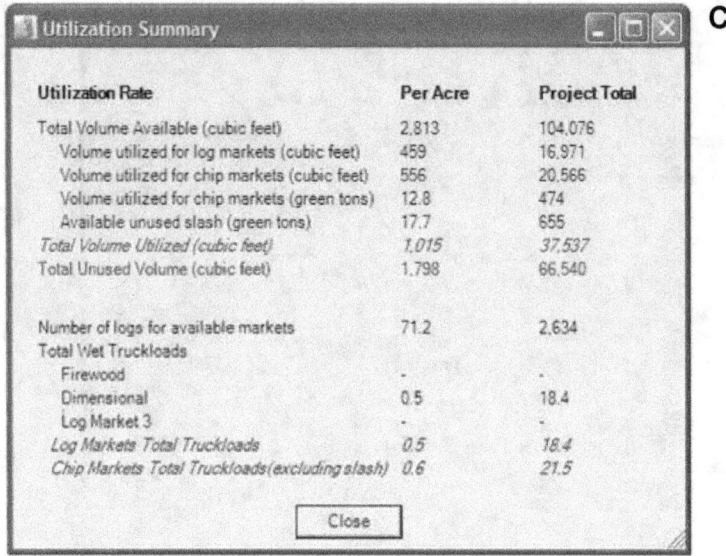

Conclusion

Total project costs and financial return are a function of a number of factors illustrated in the pervious steps, many of which may be highly variable. Because they are variable and may change substantially from one project to another, care must be taken when interpreting results. The accuracy of results is also dependent upon the quality of information entered by the user. Default inputs are provided for use where there is missing or incomplete information, but results will only be as accurate as the degree to which they reflect on-the-ground conditions. The HCR Estimator should therefore be used only to assist project planning and not as a substitute for sound business planning.

The strength of the HCR Estimator is that it allows users to assess how different market scenarios influence profitability relative to financial inputs. This provides a critical step in the development of a fully integrated system that is able to anticipate how changes in silvicultural prescription affect project costs and, in turn, the sensitivity of project costs to market factors. At every functional step, a decision is made that influences profitability. The aggregate of these decisions influences the degree to which contractors are able to effectively implement fuel reduction projects and ultimately the viability of wood products businesses; viability of such businesses is necessary to aid in reducing the risk of catastrophic wildfire on public and private lands. The HCR Estimator is an attempt to enhance estimates of harvest costs and product values, which will expedite implementation of fuel reduction projects.

Metric Equivalents

When you know:	Multiply by:	To find:
Inches (in)	2.54	Centimeters
Feet (ft)	.305	Meters
Miles (mi)	1.609	Kilometers
Miles per hour (mph)	.447	Meters per second
Acres (ac)	.405	Hectares
Square inches (in^2)	645	Square millimeters
Square feet (ft^2)	.0929	Square meters
Cubic feet (ft^3)	.0283	Cubic meters
Cubic inches (in^3)	.0000164	Cubic meters
Gallons (gal)	3.78	Liters
Pounds (lb)	.454	Kilograms
Tons (ton)	907	Kilograms
Square feet per acre (ft^2/ac)	.229	Square meters per hectare
Cubic feet per acre (ft^3/ac)	.07	Cubic meters per hectare
Trees per acre	2.47	Trees per hectare
Horsepower (hp)	.746	Kilowatts

References

Araki, D. 1994. Observations of the Peterson Pacific DDC 5000 log delimber-debarker-chipper. Tech. Note TN-214. Point-Claire, PQ: Forest Engineering Research Institute Canada (FERIC). 8 p.

Brinker, R.W.; Kinard, J.; Rummer, B.; Lanford, B. 2002. Machine rates for selected harvesting machines. Circular 296 Revised. Auburn, AL: Alabama Agricultural Experimental Station, Auburn University. 24 p.

Brown, J.K.; Snell, J.A.K.; Bunnell, D.L. 1977. Handbook for predicting slash weight of western conifers. GTR-INT-37. Ogden, UT: U.S. Department of Agriculture Forest Service Intermountain Forest and Range Experiment Station. 35 p.

Desrochers, L. 1993. Recovery of residues from delimbing and delimbing-debarking using tub grinders. Tech. Note TN-209. Point-Claire, PQ: Forest Engineering Research Institute Canada (FERIC). 8 p.

Desrochers, L. 1998. Trial of the Maxigrind 425 trailer-mounted grinder for chipping delimbing residues. Field Note 105. Point-Claire,PQ: Forest Engineering Research Institute Canada (FERIC). 2 p.

Desrochers, L.; Puttock, D.; Ryans, M. 1995. Recovery of roadside residues using drum chippers. Tech. Rep. TR-111. Point-Claire, PQ: Forest Engineering Research Institute Canada (FERIC). 18 p.

Dietz, E. 1997. Wages in forestry and logging. Compensation and Working Conditions. 1997 (Spring): 51–53.

Drews, E.S.; Hartsough, B.R.; Doyal, J.A.; Kellogg, L.D. 2001. Harvester-forwarder and harvester-yarder systems for fuels reduction treatments. International Journal of Forest Engineering. 12(1): 81–91.

Fight, R.D.; Barbour, R.J. 2005. Financial analysis of fuel treatments. PNW-GTR-662. Portland, OR: U.S. Department of Agriculture, Forest Service, Pacific Northwest Research Station. 20 p.

Hann, D.W.; Bare B. 1978. Comprehensive tree volume equations for major species of New Mexico and Arizona: I. Results and methodology. Res. Pap. INT-209. Ogden, UT: U.S. Department of Agriculture, Forest Service, Intermountain Forest and Range Experiment Station. 43 p.

Hartsough, B.R.; Drews, E.S.; McNeel, J.F.; Durston, T.A.; Stokes, B.J. 1997. Comparison of mechanized systems for thinning ponderosa pine and mixed conifer stands. Forest Products Journal. 47(11/12): 59–68.

Hartsough, B.R.; Gicqueau, A.; Fight, R.D. 1998. Productivity and cost relationships for harvesting ponderosa pine plantations. Forest Products Journal. 48(9): 87–93.

Hartsough, B.R.; Zhang, X.; Fight, R.D. 2001. Harvesting cost model for small trees in natural stands in the interior Northwest. Forest Products Journal. 51(4): 54–61.

Husch, B.; Miller, C.I.; Beers, T.W. 1982. Forest Mensuration. 3rd ed. Malabar, FL: Krieger Publishing. 456 p.

John Deere. 2003. Specifications for 850C-II LCP. http://www.deere.com/servlet/com.deere.u90785.specscompare.view.servlets. [Date accessed unknown].

Keegan, C.E.; Chase, A.L.; Morgan, T.A.; Bodmer, S.E.; Van Hooser, D.D.; Mortimer, M. 2001a. Arizona's forest products industry: a descriptive analysis 1998. Missoula, MT: University of Montana-Missoula, Bureau of Business and Economic Research. 20 p.

Keegan, C.E.; Chase, A.L.; Morgan, T.A.; Bodmer, S.E.; Van Hooser, D.D.; Mortimer, M. 2001b. New Mexico's forest products industry: a descriptive analysis 1997. Missoula, MT: University of Montana-Missoula, Bureau of Business and Economic Research. 24 p.

Kellogg, L.D.; Bettinger, P. 1994. Thinning productivity and cost for a mechanized cut-to-length system in the northwest Pacific coast region of the USA. International Journal of Forest Engineering. 5(2): 43–54.

Lambert, M.B.; Howard, J.O. 1990. Cost and productivity of new technology for harvesting and in-woods processing small diameter trees. Res. Pap. PNW-RP-430. Portland, OR: U.S. Department of Agriculture, Forest Service, Pacific Northwest Research Station. 44 p.

Larson, D.; Mirth, R. 2004. A case study on the economics of thinning in the wildland urban interface. Western Journal of Applied Forestry. 19(1): 60–65.

Lowell, E.C.; Green, D.W. 2001. Lumber recovery from small-diameter ponderosa pine from Flagstaff, Arizona. In: Vance, R.K.; Covington, W.W.; Edminster, C.B., tech. coords. Ponderosa pine ecosystems restoration: steps toward stewardship. Proceedings RMRS-P-22. Ogden, UT: U.S. Department of Agriculture, Forest Service, Rocky Mountain Research Station: 161–165.

McNeel, J.F.; Rutherford, D. 1994. Modeling harvester-forwarder system performance in a selection harvest. International Journal of Forest Engineering. 6(1): 7–14.

Miyata, E.S. 1980. Determining fixed and operating costs of logging equipment. Gen. Tech. Rep. NC-55. St. Paul, MN: U.S. Department of Agriculture, Forest Service, North Central Forest Experiment Station. 16 p.

Ostwald, P.E. 2002. Construction cost analysis and estimating. Upper Saddle River, NJ: Prentice Hall, Inc. 462 p.

Peurifoy, R.L.; Oberlender; G.D. 2002. Estimating construction costs. 5th ed. New York, NY: McGraw-Hill. 512 p.

Plummer, G.; Stokes, B. 1983. Petroleum product consumption estimators for off-highway forest operations. APA Tech. Paper. 83-A-12. Washington, DC: Southwide Energy Committee. 10 p.

PRIMEDIA Business Magazines & Media, Inc. 2003. Green guide for construction equipment. Vol. 1, 3rd Quarter. Norcross, GA. 127 p.

Raymond, K.A.; Franklin, G.S. 1990. Chain flail delimber-debarkers in eastern Canada: a preliminary assessment. Tech. Note TN-153. Point-Claire, PQ: Forest Engineering Research Institute Canada. (FERIC). 8 p.

Spelter, H.; Alderman M. 2005. Profile 2005: softwood sawmills in the United States and Canada. Res. Pap. FPL-RP-630. Madison,WI: U.S. Department of Agriculture, Forest Service, Forest Products Laboratory. 85 p.

Stokes, B.J.; Watson, W.F. 1991. Wood recovery with in-woods flailing and chipping. Tappi Journal. 74(9): 109–113.

Thompson, J.D. 2003. Productivity of a tree-length harvesting system thinning ponderosa pine in northern Arizona. Auburn, AL: U.S. Department of Agriculture, Forest Service, Southern Research Station. 5 p.

U.S. Department of Labor Employment & Training Administration. [N.d.]. Unemployment insurance tax topic. http://www.ows.doleta.gov/unemploy/uitaxtopic.asp. (December 11, 2007).

U.S. Department of Labor, Bureau of Labor Statistics. 2007. 2006 state occupational employment and wage estimates. Division of Occupational Employment Statistics. http://stats.bls.gov/oes/current/oessrcst.htm. (October 17, 2007).

Van Der Toorn, S. 2004. Personal communication. Executive Vice President, Southwest Forest Products, 2828 S 35th Ave., Phoenix, AZ 85009.

Watson, W.F.; Stokes, B.J. 1994. Final report of the Mescalero flail/chipper productivity study. Mescalero, NM: U.S. Department of the Interior, Bureau of Indian Affairs. 21 p.

Windel, K.; Bradshaw, S. 2002. Understory biomass reduction methods and equipment catalog. Tech. Rep. 0051-2826-MTDC. Missoula, MT: U.S. Department of Agriculture, Forest Service, Missoula Technology and Development Center. 156 p.

Appendix 1. Log Calculator

The Harvest Cost-Revenue (HCR) Estimator depends on an internal log calculator to determine merchantable volumes and log potential as a function of stand data and market conditions. Statistical tree profiles are used to describe the geometric attributes of each generic tree from which volume and log data are derived. Market conditions dictate size specifications of desired logs, which determine the amount of each tree that is utilized. Remaining portions of the tree not used for the selected markets, regardless of size, are assumed to be of no economic value.

Data Collection

Tree species have unique geometric profiles based upon variability in soil composition, slope, aspect, and moisture, which differ by region of the country. Profile equations for ponderosa pine (*Pinus ponderosa* Dougl. ex Laws.) in the Southwest United States were used in the HCR Estimator and were derived from tree data collected in the Flagstaff, Arizona, wildland-urban interface by Lowell and Green (2001) and compared to previous research by Hann and Bare (1978). Information collected for 6-in to 16-in diameter at breast height (DBH) trees included tree age, total tree height, height to start of live crown, height to 6-in top, height to 4-in top, stump height, butt log top and bottom diameter inside bark (DIB), butt log length and its bark thickness, top and bottom DIB of top log, top log length and its bark thickness.

Average age of the 152 sampled trees was 89.6 years with a standard deviation of 11.0 years. No relationship was detected between tree age and tree DBH. There was, however, a strongly correlated estimate of butt log diameter as a function of tree DBH (fig. 14) that was used in the log calculator function of the model. A correlation was also found of white wood taper with tree DBH: larger trees experience greater taper over their height than do smaller trees (fig. 15).

The log calculator also makes use of a tree height to tree DBH relationship obtained through the analysis of a larger data set (n = 11,522) of unpublished research collected by the Ecological Restoration Institute, Northern Arizona University [1] in the same locations as the Lowell and Green (2001) data. This tree height, *H* (ft) to DBH (in), relationship is given by equation 1.

$$H = 100 - 97.12e^{-.0638DBH} \quad R^2 = 0.7843 \tag{1}$$

---

[1] Fulé, P.Z. 2000. Tree height-diameter data from units 5, 6, and 7, Fort Valley Research and Demonstration Project. Unpublished data. On file with: Ecological Restoration Institute, Northern Arizona University, Flagstaff, AZ 86011.

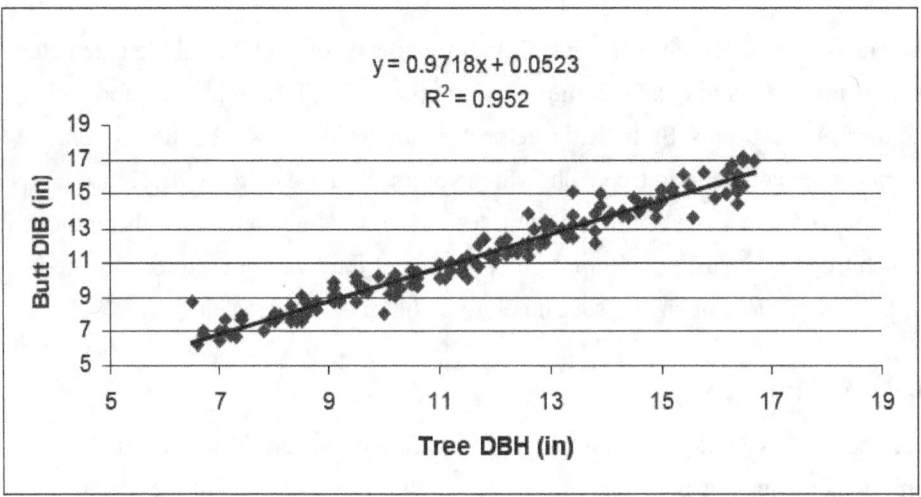

Figure 14—Estimating butt end diameter inside bark (DIB) from diameter at breast height (DBH) for ponderosa pine trees from Flagstaff, Arizona.

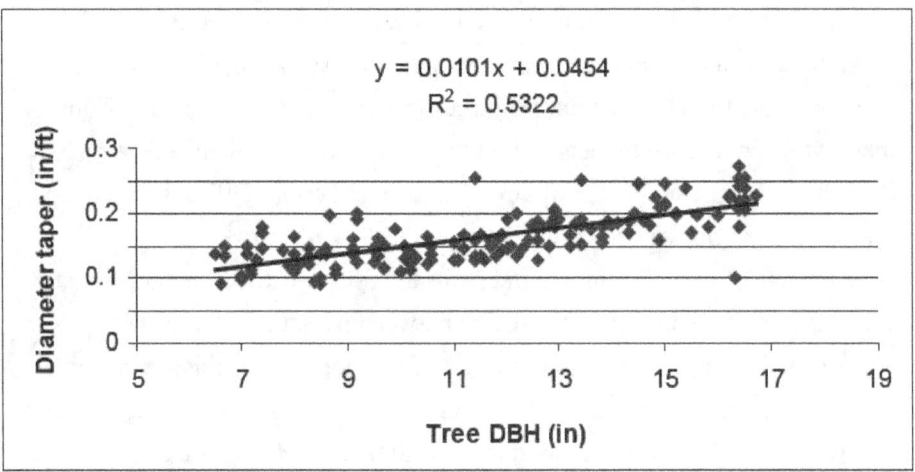

Figure 15—White wood diameter taper by tree diameter breast height (DBH) for ponderosa pine trees, Flagstaff, Arizona.

Figure 16 provides a comparison between the collected heights of the Lowell and Green (2001) trees and heights predicted by equation 1.

Extracting Merchantable Logs

The log calculator estimates the possible number of logs and merchantable volume per tree from the user-specified cut-tree list (step 1) for a specified cutting unit. The first set of calculations establishes the basic whole-tree-log (WTLog) parameters necessary for market-by-market log extractions. An example of these calculations is provided in table 2 for cut-tree data taken from a sample plot of ponderosa pine

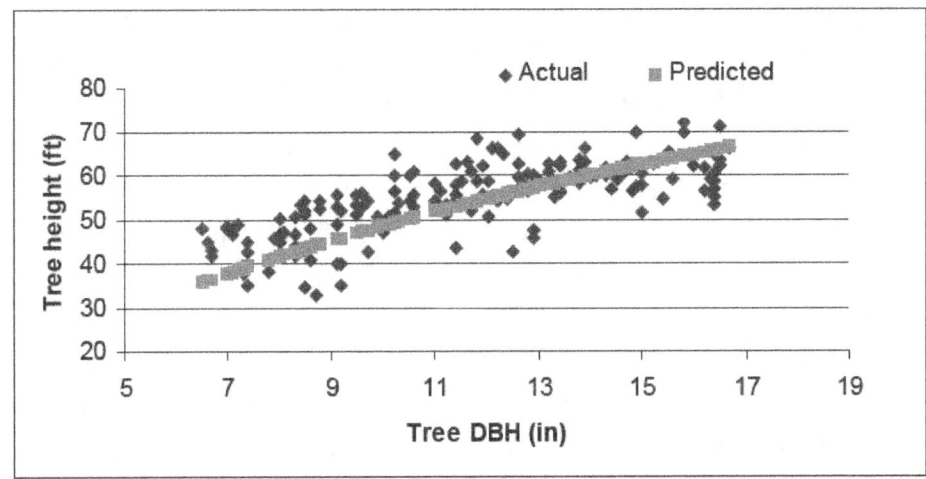

Figure 16—Actual and predicted tree height by diameter breast height (DBH) for ponderosa pine trees, Flagstaff, Arizona.

Table 2—Whole-tree log calculations per tree (4-inch top) for sample plot cut-tree data

DBH class	Cut trees	Height	Basal area	Butt diameter inside bark	White wood diameter taper	Length to top	Volume to top
Inches	*Per acre*	*Feet*	*ft²*	*Inches*	*in/ft*	*Feet*	*ft³*
1	12.6	8.88	0.01	1.02	0.0555	0.00	0.00
2	6.9	14.51	0.02	2.00	0.0656	0.00	0.00
3	6.9	19.80	0.05	2.97	0.0757	0.00	0.00
4	10.9	24.76	0.09	3.94	0.0858	0.00	0.00
5	11.7	29.41	0.14	4.91	0.0959	9.50	1.03
6	8.1	33.77	0.20	5.88	0.106	17.77	2.39
7	10.1	37.86	0.27	6.85	0.1161	24.59	4.04
8	15.4	41.70	0.35	7.83	0.1262	30.32	5.98
9	15.4	45.31	0.44	8.80	0.1363	35.21	8.23
10	10.5	48.69	0.55	9.77	0.1464	39.41	10.79
11	12.1	51.86	0.66	10.74	0.1565	43.08	13.66
12	8.1	54.83	0.79	11.71	0.1666	46.30	16.84
13	9.7	57.63	0.92	12.69	0.1767	49.16	20.35
14	8.5	60.24	1.07	13.66	0.1868	51.70	24.17
15	4.9	62.70	1.23	14.63	0.1969	53.98	28.32
16	0	0	0	0	0	0	0
17	0.4	67.17	1.58	16.57	0.2171	57.91	37.58

DBH = diameter at breast height.

trees in the Fort Valley Experimental Forest in Flagstaff, Arizona. The column-by-column results include column 3 tree height, column 4 basal area, column 5 butt DIB estimated from the regression equation of figure 14, column 6 white wood diameter taper estimated from the regression equation of figure 15, column 7 *WTLogLength* to a user-specified top, and column 8 WTLog volume calculated for the same top. These calculations are performed for each DBH class and give results per tree. The *WTLogLength* in column 7 is the total tree length (in feet) from stump to top calculated by using equation 2, which is a function of top and butt DIB divided by the white wood diameter taper (in/ft) (*WWDiaTaper*). Column 8 is the volume in cubic feet (cf) that the WTLog represents determined by using Newton's formula, as shown in equation 3, where mid-log diameter is estimated as the average of the butt DIB and top DIB (in inches). Newton's formula is applicable to neiloids, cones, and parabolic frustums and gives the best results, in comparison to other geometric formulas, for all sections of the tree except for butt logs with excessive swell (Husch et al. 1982).

$$WTLogLength(ft) = \frac{ButtDIB - TopDIB}{WWDiaTaper} \qquad (2)$$

$$WTLogVol = \frac{\pi(WTLogLength)^2}{576}\left\{(ButtDIB)^2 + 4\left[\frac{(ButtDia+TopDia)}{2}\right]^2 + (TopDIB)^2\right\} \qquad (3)$$

The log market information provided by the user is combined with the WTLog results to determine the merchantable log potential of cut trees. The log calculator can accept up to three distinctly different log markets. The small-end log DIB specification defines log size. Because a geometric progression is assumed, the log calculator cannot handle markets where the log diameters overlap. The extraction assumes that the largest diameter log is the priority market, and cut trees are examined to produce this log first. Remaining log lengths not suitable for the largest log market are placed in intermediate and smaller log markets. Figure 17 shows a graphical representation of how the log calculator extracts three different market logs from a hypothetical WTLog.

WTLogLength and *WTLogVol* are estimated based on user inputs of tree DBH. The length from butt DIB to small-end DIB is determined by using equation 4 to test whether a tree can yield a merchantable log for a particular market. In a three-log market scenario, the distance from the WTLog butt end to the user-specified log big end is calculated by using equation 5. The *LengthtoBigEnd* value represents the length of tree adjacent to the stump that is too big in diameter to be utilized by the log market. By comparing the *LengthtoSmallEnd* to *LengthtoBigEnd*, the log calculator determines whether or not the tree is capable of yielding a log meeting

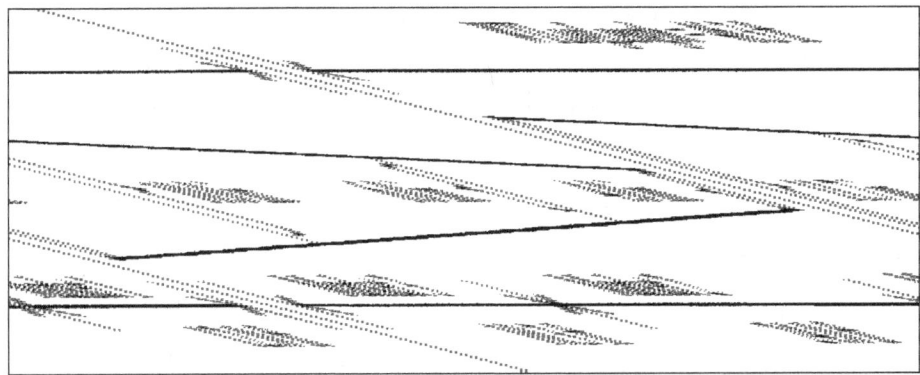

Figure 17—Log length and sizes cut from a 12-inch diameter breast height tree for a hypothetical three-log market.

at least one of the log market specifications giving priority to the largest possible log first. A tree produces at least one log if the difference in *LengthtoSmallEnd* and *LengthtoBigEnd* is greater than or equal to the minimum log length input by the user. A tree can produce two logs if the difference is greater than two minimum log lengths. If the difference is less than the minimum specified value for any log market, the tree does not yield a marketable log.

$$LengthtoSmallEnd(ft) \quad \frac{ButtDIB \quad LogSmallEndDIB}{WWDiaTaper} \qquad (4)$$

$$LengthtoBigEnd(ft) \quad \frac{ButtDIB \quad LogBigEndDIB}{WWDiaTaper} \qquad (5)$$

The available length for the second largest-sized log market is calculated by subtracting the length used for the largest-sized log market from WTLog length to top. As above, the log calculator determines the number of logs that meet user-specified market conditions for this second market. The number of logs available to the remaining market using the smallest logs is then determined based on the remaining WTLog length not utilized by the first market with largest logs or the second market with mid-sized logs. The number of merchantable logs per acre is obtained by multiplying the number of viable logs per tree per DBH class for each of the three markets by the number of cut trees in that DBH class per acre.

To demonstrate, the log calculator predicted that 114.9 trees of the 152.2 cut trees per acre (TPA) from the sample plot in table 2 were merchantable in at least one of the three user-defined markets depicted in figure 17. The 114.9 merchantable TPA yielded 231.5 merchantable logs/acre because some trees yielded multiple logs, of which 114.9 logs/acre went to the smallest-sized log market, 85 logs/acre went to the mid-sized log market, and 31.5 logs/acre went to largest-sized log market. All merchantable trees were fully utilized except for the 7-in and 11-in DBH trees that each had unused volume. The 5-in DBH trees were the smallest to yield a merchantable log, a 9.5-ft long by 4-in small-end diameter log. The remaining 36.8 TPA were too small to be utilized in this hypothetical three-log market scenario.

Estimating Number of Truckloads

The log calculator then uses the estimate of the number of logs available per market and corresponding log size to estimate the number of truckloads of logs per market. The number of logs per truckload and the number of truckloads per acre are limited by either total legal load weight or total log volume. The weight is estimated by calculating the total green weight of available logs per market per acre as shown in equation 6, and the number of truckloads based on weight per acre shown in equation 7. Wet weight moisture content (*MC*) is the average green ton moisture content expressed in decimal form. *LogVol/Acre* is the volume of logs in ft^3 generated per acre.

$$\frac{Tons}{Acre} \quad \frac{\left[24.96\,\frac{lbs}{ft^3}\,(1+MC)\,\frac{LogVol}{Acre}\right]}{2{,}000\,\frac{lbs}{ton}} \tag{6}$$

$$\frac{Loads_{wt}}{Acre} \quad \frac{Tons/Acre}{26\,tons/load} \tag{7}$$

Volume limit is estimated by calculating the number of logs per load based on the cross-sectional area of a semi-trailer bunk filled with stacked logs as shown in equation 8 and the number of truckloads based on volume per acre shown in equation 9. The dimensions of a truck trailer bunk of logs are approximated as 8.5-ft wide by 9-ft high, yielding a cross-sectional area of 76.5-ft^2. The equivalent cross-sectional area of one average log within a bunk of logs is taken as a square with a side equal to the big end DIB plus 1.4 in to account for bark thickness. The governing number of loads per acre per market is taken as the maximum of either the loads per acre based on weight or the loads per acre based on volume.

$$\frac{Logs}{Load} \quad \frac{76.5\,ft^2}{(bigdib+1.4\,in)^2 \Big/ 144\frac{in^2}{ft^2}} \tag{8}$$

$$\frac{Loads_{vol}}{Acre} \quad \frac{Logs/Acre}{Logs/Load} \tag{9}$$

Appendix 2. Biomass Calculator

In addition to the log calculator, the Harvest Cost-Revenue (HCR) Estimator uses an internal biomass calculator to determine chip and slash volume as a function of stand data and market conditions. Statistical tree profile data presented in appendix 1 are used to describe the geometric attributes of each tree from which chip and slash data are derived. Where both log and chip markets are selected, market specifications for logs dictate remaining available volume for wood chips. The HCR Estimator prioritizes allocation of total available volume to log markets first. Remaining portions of the tree not used for the selected log markets are allocated to chip markets based on chip market specifications.

Wood chips are classified by the part of the tree processed. Clean chips are free of most bark, branches, needles, and other impurities and include only bole wood, which is the white wood from the tree base to the specified top diameter inside bark (DIB). Bole weight (*bole*) is calculated by using the volume obtained from Newton's formula in equation 3. Dirty chips include bole wood as well as slash, where slash is the combination of bark and tree crown. Bark weight (*bark*) is estimated from equations generated by Brown et al. (1977) from ponderosa pine (*Pinus ponderosa* Dougl. ex Laws.) samples in Idaho and Montana and verified with trees sampled in Arizona by Lowell and Green (2001). Total crown weight (*crown*), which is the aggregation of all needles, twigs, and tree tips, is also estimated from values taken from Brown and colleagues (1977) for log small-end DIB of 3, 4, and 6-inches.

Total clean or dirty chip weight from a project site is determined by the amount of slash and bole wood recovered from the skidding, chipping, or grinding process. Stokes and Watson (1991) estimated that 15.6 percent of slash is lost as unrecoverable from felling and skidding when using a whole-tree harvesting system. For the HCR Estimator, slash recovery is less than 84.4 percent for any type of harvesting system modeled. Loss from chipping is also estimated from values obtained by Stokes and Watson (1991). For clean and dirty chips, flail chain loss is estimated at 15.10 percent of total chips, and for clean chips only, screening reject is 4.90 percent. Clean (*CC*) and dirty chip (*DC*) weights are calculated by using equations 10 and 11, respectively.

$$CC \ (lbs/tree) \quad bole \times [1 \quad (15.10 + 4.90)] \qquad (10)$$

$$DC \ (lbs/tree) \quad (bole + bark + crown) \times [1 \quad (15.10)] \qquad (11)$$

Similar to the log market specifications, users may designate a minimum size tree to be utilized for clean or dirty chip markets. All unutilized trees are piled in the woods for burning, lopped and scattered in the woods, pulverized with a masticator, or left standing for tree recruitment.

Appendix 3. Equipment Cost Estimator

Ownership Costs

The cost of equipment activities in the Harvest Cost-Revenue (HCR) Estimator includes ownership and operating costs. Ownership costs are calculated by using a traditional cost accounting approach documented by Miyata (1980) that includes initial purchase price, annual depreciation, opportunity cost, and insurance.

Purchase Price

Initial purchase price (*P*) per equipment piece is determined in one of two ways: (1) reported new or used equipment purchase price paid by the owner, plus applicable sales taxes; (2) price estimated as a function of engine horsepower to new purchase price (Brinker et al. 2002). If the price paid by the owner is unknown, purchase price is estimated by using new equipment prices documented in the *Green Guide* (PRIMEDIA Business Magazines & Media, Inc. 2003) and Circular 296 (Brinker et al. 2002). The regression equations in table 3 are used to calculate new purchase price.

Annual Depreciation

Annual depreciation (*AD*) costs are determined by using a straight-line schedule with an assumed economic life (*N*) of 5 years and an equipment salvage value (*S*) equal to 20 percent of the initial investment price (*P*). Used equipment is assumed to have a renewed economic life of 5 years at every purchase regardless of equipment age. Annual depreciation is calculated according to equation 12.

$$AD = \frac{P - S}{N} \qquad (12)$$

Opportunity Costs

Annual opportunity cost reflects the loss of investment interest that the money spent toward the initial equipment purchase could have yielded. This cost is estimated to equal 7 percent of the average yearly investment (*AYI*). Economic life of equipment renews with every purchase, new or used, so that annual cost of investment can be calculated over the lifetime of the loan, assumed to be 5 years. The average value of yearly investment is calculated according to equation 13.

$$AYI = \frac{(P - S)(N + 1)}{2N} + S \qquad (13)$$

Table 3—Regression equations for determining purchase price of equipment when the price paid by owner is unknown

Equipment	New purchase price (P) regression equation	Valid horsepower range
	Dollars	*hp*
Cut-to-length harvester	P = 777.51 hp + 220,050	150–260
Forwarder	P = 1,545.5 hp + 19,101	100–260
Feller-buncher (wheeled)	P = 1,050.7 hp + 9,549	100–260
Feller-buncher (tracked)	P = 1,443.9 hp + 31,348	130–260
Grapple skidder (wheeled)	P = 1,164.6 hp – 186	115–260
Grapple skidder (tracked)	P = 2,970.7 hp – 113,775	105–155
Stroke-delimber	Limited observations	225
Loader (front-end wheeled)	P = 2,410.8 hp – 161,640	110–230
Loader (front-end tracked)	P = 1,250.0 hp + 112,321	130–350
Spotting tractor	P = 198.08 hp – 28,231	210–250
Dozer	P = 1,751.8 hp – 19,841	80–130
Delimber-debarker-chipper	P = 562.69 hp + 78,976	455–1,000
Whole-tree chipper (self-propelled)	P = 473.5 hp + 52,894	275–760
Whole-tree chipper (towable)	P = 396.31 hp + 15,916	275–1,000
Grinder	P = 431.13 hp + 52,691	395–860

Insurance

The cost to insure equipment against loss (i) is estimated as a percentage of *AYI* where i is uniquely assigned to each machine according to the rates found in Brinker et al. (2002).

Total annual ownership costs are converted to hourly costs to determine the proportional share of equipment ownership costs. Total number of hours worked over the course of 1 year, known as scheduled machine hours (SMH), is also necessary to calculate hourly costs. For example, 10 total months of harvesting operations at 40 hours per week equates to 1,800 SMH.

Operating Costs

Operating costs are accrued as the direct result of using the equipment, which changes in proportion to the number of actual hours used. Operating costs include the following:

Maintenance and Repair

Maintenance and repair costs are estimated as a percentage of AD (Brinker et al. 2002) and differ depending on type of equipment. For equipment that has surpassed its economic life, maintenance and repair costs are assumed to remain equal to the original percentage of AD. Maintenance and repair costs include preventative care, parts, labor, tire or track replacement, and related costs associated with using equipment. It should be noted that as equipment ages, it may incur maintenance and repair costs greater than estimated in the model, but those costs will vary substantially based on use rates, preventative maintenance, harvest conditions, and other factors.

Fuel Consumption and Lubricants

Fuel consumption costs are estimated by using consumption rates unique to each machine multiplied by off-highway fuel price per gallon. Consumption rates are derived from Brinker et al. (2002) and Plummer and Stokes (1983). Engine oil, hydraulic oil, and other costs for lubricants and filters are determined as a percentage of fuel costs. A rate of 36.8 percent of hourly fuel cost is used (Brinker et al. 2002, Plummer and Stokes 1983).

Total annual operating costs are converted to hourly costs for the purpose of assigning to the respective project its proportional share of the equipment operating costs. Total number of hours the contractor assumes to be actually using the equipment for its intended purpose, known as productive machine hours (PMH), is necessary to calculate hourly costs. The PMH is calculated by multiplying SMH by a machine utilization rate. Utilization rates are unique to each machine and are estimated according to the rates found in Brinker et al. (2002). For example, considering time spent for daily equipment maintenance, refueling, lunch, and rest breaks, a whole-tree feller buncher may be used to harvest trees at a rate of 60 percent of SMH. Assuming 1,800 SMH, total PMH hours would be 1,080 per year.

Productivity and Activity Costs

Equipment productivity was used to estimate the total amount of time necessary to perform functions. Ownership and operating costs are assigned based on the total estimated project time for each piece of equipment. Equipment productivity was determined, where applicable, from previously published empirical studies and modified via field observations and data collected by using time-motion sampling in the Southwest. Time-motion sampling involves the observation and recording of the time required to complete predetermined activities unique to each piece of equipment. Regression equations were developed for equipment and compared against the published literature.

System productivity is further determined based on the system balance, which is the lowest productive machine time for a particular operation. The machine with the lowest productivity controls the sequencing of the follow-on machines and, most important for cost estimating, it establishes the operating time for each piece of equipment from which operating costs are calculated.

Handfelling

Productivity for handfelling trees with chain saws was determined from time-motion data collected in four locations on A-1 Mountain of the Coconino National Forest in northern Arizona during the fall of 2002. Time necessary to fell trees 6 in diameter breast height (DBH) or greater was recorded for 104 ponderosa pine (*Pinus ponderosa* Dougl. ex Laws.) trees. Productivity was also recorded for submerchantable trees less than 6 in DBH, which was determined by market availability. Submerchantable aspects consisted of cutting the unmarked trees less than 6 in and lopping the slash to a height of less than 2 ft. The average size of merchantable trees was 10.1-in DBH, and the average number of merchantable trees cut was 74 trees per acre (TPA).

Productivity for trees greater than 6 in was recorded for the time to walk between trees, felling, bucking merchantable logs, and delimbing. Time per tree for trees less than 6 in was a function of felling and walking. Break time, which included time for refueling, sharpening and tightening chains, lunch, and water breaks, averaged 94 seconds/tree for merchantable logs. Table 4 displays total time broken down by function for logs greater than and less than 6 in.

Time-motion study results were compared to Hartsough et al. (1998, 2001). Hartsough et al. (1998) derived a relationship for predicting productivity in terms of ccf [100 ft^3] per productive man-hour for the combined handfelling, delimbing, and bucking activities. This derivation came from empirical observations made in a 1972 study in young-growth mixed-conifer stands in north-central California that was modified to reflect enhanced chain-sawing technology in accordance with observations made in a 1987 study in coastal second-growth timber. When applied to the unit 273 data, the resulting time per acre was significantly less than observed times.

Table 4—Productivity data by function for trees based on diameter at breast height (DBH)

	Trees 6-in DBH or larger				Trees less than 6-in DBH			
	Unit 273	Unit 274	Unit 322	Unit 323	Unit 273	Unit 274	Unit 322	Unit 323
Trees cut per acre (TPA)	103.2	44.8	—	—	49.0	32.8	57.3	38.9
Average DBH cut (in)	10.1	10.1	—	—	—	—	—	—
Felling (min/ac)	42.39	18.19	—	—	8.06	5.09	11.74	8.40
Delimb and buck (min/ac)	146.19	62.73	—	—	—	—	—	—
Walk (min/ac)	33.05	14.18	—	—	12.65	10.64	13.55	11.44
Total productive time (min/ac)	221.63	95.10	—	—	20.71	15.72	25.29	19.84

— = no data.

Felling time was estimated by using equation 14—a relationship derived by Hartsough et al. (2001). Walking time per tree was approximated by equation 15 using an average distance walked per tree of 208.7 ft and a walking speed of 132 ft/min derived from the A-1 Mountain study. Total handfelling time was further estimated per acre by using equation 16.

$$Felling\ Time\ (^{min}\!/_{tree})\quad 0.1+ 0.0111DBH^{1.496} \qquad (14)$$

$$Walking\ Time\ (^{min}\!/_{tree})\quad \frac{208.7\,ft\left(1+\sqrt{tpa}\right)}{132\,^{ft}\!/_{min}} \qquad (15)$$

$$Total\ Handfelling\ Time\ (^{min}\!/_{acre})\quad \frac{WalkingTime^{0.5}\,(208.7 + 208.7)}{132 + Felling\ Time\ Per\ Acre} \qquad (16)$$

Cut-To-Length (CTL) Harvester

The CTL harvester does all the processing (harvesting, delimbing, and bucking) in the woods and is able to fell multiple trees from the same location depending on equipment reach and tree density. One harvester cycle includes positioning the machine to cut a tree, felling, processing limbs and bucking to the desired length, piling or sorting logs in the woods, and moving to the next set of trees. Production equations used in the model were determined by reviewing Drews et al. (2001), Hartsough and colleagues (1997, 1998, 2001), Kellogg and Bettinger (1994), and McNeel and Rutherford (1994). Hartsough et al. (1997) was determined to be the most applicable when using the following assumptions: based on observations made by Thompson (2003), distance of machine movement between activity sets (cycles) was set equal to 15 ft, and trail spacing was set at 50 ft. However, it should be noted that distance between equipment sets will be highly variable, depending on tree spacing, harvest prescriptions, and obstacles.

Harvester productivity was quantified for a Timberjack 1270 harvester with 762B head for trees down to 2 in diameter. Productivity was measured for 408 machine cycles. The CTL harvester relationship given in equation 17 (*CTLProcess-Time*) from Hartsough et al. (1997) reflects the various activities in one cycle, where *Slope* is the average ground slope across the project area and *CutTPA* is the number of merchantable trees harvested per acre for the defined markets.

$$CTLProcessTime\ (^{min}\!/_{acre}) =$$
$$\frac{76.11 - 8.31DBH + 0.63DBH^2 + 0.1974Slope + 20.904Slope}{CutTPA} \qquad (17)$$

Forwarder

A CTL harvesting system generally includes the CTL harvester and a forwarder. The forwarder moves the processed logs, and sometimes the generated slash, to a roadside landing or to a waiting trailer for transport out of the woods. One cycle time includes unloaded travel time, loading time, intermediate travel time, loaded travel, and unloading time. Stand and system variables such as stem size, slope, and extraction distance were used to predict machine productivity. Production relationships were determined by examining Drews et al. (2001) and Hartsough et al. (1998), which relied on Hartsough et al. (1997) and McNeel and Rutherford (1994). Hartsough et al. (1998) was determined to be the most appropriate. The forwarder relationship given in equation 18 (*ForwarderCycleTime*) reflects the various activities in one cycle for a Timberjack 1010 forwarder, where *loadVol* is the total volume in cubic feet per forward bunk, *logsPerLoad* is the total logs per bunk, and *logsPerTree* is the total number of viable logs per tree.

$$ForwarderCycleTime\ (^{min}\!/_{acre}) =$$
$$\left(1179.3(^{min}\!/_{load}) + 9.48LogsPerLoad\right) + 0.485\left(^{43,560loadVol}\!/_{50CutTPA \times AveVol}\right) \qquad (18)$$
$$+ 2.79\left(^{Slope}\!/_{logsPerLoad \times logsPerTree \times CutTPA}\right)$$

Whole-Tree Feller-Buncher

The whole-tree feller-buncher fells and piles trees in the woods. One harvester cycle includes move-to-tree, fell, move-to-dump, and pile. Production relationships used in the model were determined by reviewing Hartsough and colleagues (1997, 1998, 2001) and Thompson (2003). Thompson (2003) was determined to be the most applicable but was modified by using Hartsough et al. (1997) to estimate the number of trees per cycle, and Hartsough et al. (1998) to adjust for ground slope.

Conventional whole-tree harvesting productivity was quantified for a Hydro-ax 421E drive-to-tree feller-buncher. Harvesting productivity was measured for 409 machine cycles (935 trees) and tree data were recorded for 157 cycles. The average number of trees per cycle was 2.45 with an average DBH of 8.6 in. The average total cycle time per tree was 16.43 seconds equating to 220 trees per hour. The regression analysis indicated that the number of trees per cycle and the basal area per cycle best predicted time per tree. The whole-tree feller-buncher relationship given in equation 19 (*WTFellerBunch*) reflects the various activities in one cycle.

$$WTFellerBunch \left(^{min}\!/_{cycle}\right)=$$

$$0.395\left(^{min}\!/_{tree}\right) + 0.0304DBH\left(\frac{CutTPA}{2\,98-0\,0664DBH+\left(0\,364\!/_{DBH}\right)-0\,0058Slope}\right) \quad (19)$$

Grapple Skidder

Skidding is the process of picking up trees or logs that are scattered in the forest and moving them to a pile at the landing. One skidder cycle includes traveling to the logs, collecting a grapple load of logs, traveling back to the landing, and then stacking the logs into a pile at the landing. Skidding productivity was assessed by comparing a number of published equations and observations from units 273 and 274 on A-1 Mountain. Hartsough et al. (1997) derived skidding relationships from a hybrid whole-tree and cut-to-length system in California where merchantable ponderosa pine trees were processed in the woods and skidded to a landing with a Timberjack 450B and a Caterpillar 528. Thompson (2003) evaluated a Caterpillar 528 grapple skidder in northern Arizona for ponderosa pine trees in a fuel reduction treatment. Watson and Stokes (1994) evaluated a Timberjack 450 and a 380 rubber-tired grapple skidder in New Mexico for ponderosa pine and mixed conifers on moderate slopes to steep slopes. Skidding relationships developed by Watson and Stokes (1994) were deemed most robust for number of observations, slopes evaluated, and size of trees harvested. A regression equation was constructed to predict total cycle time on slopes averaging 17 percent. The skidding relationship given in equation 20 (*SkiddingCycleTime*) reflects the various activities within one cycle. *SkidDistance* is the total distance trees are moved from the last bundle of trees to the landing. *NumberBundles* is the total number of bundles of trees per acre.

$$SkiddingCycleTime\left(^{min}\!/_{acre}\right) =$$
$$0.00477(^{rate}\!/_{slope})(SkidDistance) + 1.11(^{min}\!/_{bundle})(NumberBundles) \qquad (20)$$

Stroke Delimber

Productivity for delimbing trees at the landing was examined for Drews et al. (2001), Hartsough et al. (1998, 2001), and Thompson (2003). Thompson (2003) was selected for productivity relationships given as an expression for the entire range of delimbing activity within ponderosa pine stands in the Southwest. Delimbing is a function of tree species with unique crown and limb characteristics. Other published sources give equations for non-ponderosa pine trees.

Thompson (2003) observed delimbing of 218 ponderosa pine trees with an average DBH of 10.5 in and a maximum of 19.6 in. The number of logs processed from each tree (*LogsPerTree*) ranged from 1 to 4 with an average of 1.43. The average total time per delimbing cycle was 40.83 second, which yields productivity of 88 trees/hour. The stroke delimber relationship given in equation 21 (*DelimbingCycleTime*) reflects the various activities in one cycle, including reach, process, stack, clear, and move. Total processing time per acre is calculated by multiplying the processing time per tree times the number of trees per acre.

$$DelimbingCycleTime\left(^{min}\!/_{tree}\right) =$$
$$20.19437(LogsPerTree) + 0.1112(DBH^2) - 1.2689 \qquad (21)$$

Front-End Loader

Productivity for log loading was calculated by using a combination of observed production relationships from the A-1 study site (see appendix 1) and published literature. In Hartsough et al. (1998), a simple equation is presented where loading time is directly related to tree DBH. This equation was derived using a 1969 large-log ponderosa pine study and a 1973 smaller log southern pine study. When applied to A-1 data, the equation yields an average load time per log of 33 seconds. In comparison, field observations of truck loading displayed below for units 273 and

274 yielded an average productive load time per log of 19.72 seconds. Hartsough et al. (1997) provided a loading relationship derived from observations of a Prentice 610 loading logs in a ponderosa pine plantation and a natural mixed-conifer stand, which yielded 2.11 logs/grapple and a productive time/log of 32 seconds. Their equation is modified here from load time per grapple (min) to load time per log in seconds and is restated as equation 22.

$$Load\left(\frac{sec}{log}\right) = \frac{21.06 + 21.66 \times \frac{Logs}{Grapple} - 1.87\left(\frac{Logs}{Grapple}\right)^2 + 0.089 \times \frac{Vol}{Grapple}}{\frac{Logs}{Grapple}} \tag{22}$$

Results were comparable to observations in the A-1 study. Those observations were made of a John Deere TC 544 wheeled loader with brush rake for a total of 11 truckloads. Average logs per grapple, average logs per truckload, total time loading, and time traveled between piles was recorded. The total load time per acre is calculated by multiplying the load time per log times the number of logs per acre. Equation 22 when applied to units 273 and 274 data yields an average load time per log of 19.60 sec. Equation 22 depends heavily on the number of logs per grapple, which was set at four for all units observed; the average load time per log changes only slightly ranging between 19.58 and 19.60 seconds per log. A summary of loading observations is provided in table 5.

Spotting Tractor

Spotting tractors are generally retired military trucks used to move (spot) log trailers from project sites to a convenient roadside location for highway trucks to easily access, thus increasing overall time efficiency of log transportation. The production rate for spot tractors is based simply on the number of miles traveled and the speed

Table 5—Summary of loading observations

	Units 273 and 274
Number of truckloads	11
Total number of logs	1,209
Average logs/truckload	109.91
Average logs/loader grapple	3.91
Average load time/truck (sec)	2,167
Average load time/log (sec)	19.72
Travel between piles (sec)	1,418

of travel. Time per load is estimated according to equation 23 where 0.5 hour represents the time to hook up and release the loaded trailers. For observations made in the A-1 study (app. 1), the average distance from the landing to the staging area for all four units was 3 mi, travel speed while loaded was 10 mph, and travel speed unloaded was 25 mph. Observations for the spotting tractor are displayed in table 6. These assumptions combined with equation 23 yielded an estimated time to stage each trailer of 0.92 hours.

$$Spotting\ Tractor\ \left({}^{hrs}\!/_{load}\right) = \frac{2 \times Distance\ (mi)}{[Loaded\ speed\ (mph) + Unloaded\ speed\ (mph)]} + 0.5hr \qquad (23)$$

Delimber-Debarker-Chipper (DDC)

The DDC is used to process clean chips for biomass markets, where the bark, limbs, and branches are removed prior to chipping. Productivity was determined by reviewing Araki (1994), Lambert and Howard (1990), and Raymond and Franklin (1990). A range of DDC productivity was assessed. Lambert and Howard (1990) was determined to be the most applicable by comparing total cycle time to field observations of DDC operations in eastern Arizona in 2004 for ponderosa pine, which were similar for similar-sized equipment. Average productivity was estimated as 30.0 green tons/per machine hour (MH) for clean chipping.

Table 6—Production rate observations for the spotting tractor

	Units 273 and 274
Average miles to stage	3
Speed loaded (mph)	10
Speed unloaded (mph)	25
Hook-up time per trailer (hrs)	0.25
Release time per trailer (hrs)	0.25
Time per load (hrs)	0.92
Number of loads/acre	1.44
Time per acre (hrs)	1.33

Whole-Tree Chipper

The whole-tree chipper processes the whole tree, including the bole, limbs, branches, bark, and needles for dirty chips. Whole-tree chipper productivity is estimated as a function of size and loader capacity. Production equations used in the model were determined by reviewing Desrochers et al. (1995) and Lambert and Howard (1990). Lambert and Howard (1990) was determined to be the most applicable. Productivity was estimated for a drum chipping head and attached Prentice loader in chipping mixed-conifer stands. Average productivity was 52.9 green tons/MH when the chipper was used without the debarker to produce hogged fuel.

Tub Grinder

The tub grinder differs from chipping in that resulting material resembles strands of wood as opposed to uniform chips. Grinder productivity is estimated as a function of tub size, horsepower, loader capacity, and average number of delays resulting from bridging of material in the tub or plugging. Work by Desrochers (1993 and 1998) was examined for applicability to the Southwest. Desrochers 1998 was determined to be most applicable for productivity estimates for a Maxigrind 425 trailer-mounted grinder with a separate Dresser P-71 tracked loader. Average productivity was estimated as 8.7 oven-dried tons (odt) per MH, which was determined by converting green slash to oven-dried weights. By eliminating delays owing to the front-end loader, productivity averaged 11.3 odt/MH. However, productivity may vary greatly depending on size of trees, preprocessing with a DDC, use of attached or separate loader, and whether residuals are green or dry.

Mastication

Few published studies exist on mastication, which is the pulverizing of trees with a masticator. Therefore, productivity is determined by user inputs as a function of machine costs per hour multiplied by estimated machine time per acre.

Dozer

The dozer is used for in-woods machine piling of residual slash. Machine piling is estimated as a function of dozer blade capacity (size), dozer speed, slope, and push distance. There is minimal research published on dozer productivity so it was estimated by using observations from units 273 and 274 on A-1 Mountain (see app. 1 "Data Collection"). Blade capacity for the John Deere 850C was 5.78 yd^3 (John Deere 2003). Dozer speed to collect and push slash into piles was set equal to 162.8 ft/min, maximum push distance to a pile was 75 ft (Van Der Toorn 2004), machine utilization was assumed as 60 percent (Brinker et al. 2002), and the length of an average work day was 10 hours. A summary of observed productivity is given in table 7 for residual slash from limbs and tops of merchantable trees, and for trees too small for chip or log markets that are felled for in-woods piling and burning (assumed 3-in DBH). These results compare well to the anecdotal data supplied by Van Der Toorn (2004) and machine rates compiled in Windel and Bradshaw (2002). Equations 24 through 28 are provided to calculate dozer productivity for the region.

$$Collect\ (\tfrac{min}{ac}) = \frac{208.7\,ft \times \left(1 + \sqrt{tpa}\right)}{Collect\ Speed\ (\tfrac{ft}{min})} \qquad (24)$$

$$Blades\ (\tfrac{1}{ac}) \quad \frac{Slash\ Volume\left(yd^3/ac\right)}{Blade\ Volume\ (yd^3)/4} \qquad (25)$$

$$Push\ (\tfrac{min}{ac}) = \frac{\tfrac{Blades}{ac} \times 75 \times 2}{Push\ Speed\left(\tfrac{ft}{min}\right)} \qquad (26)$$

$$Piling\ (\tfrac{hrs}{ac}) \quad \left(Collect + Push\right)/60 \qquad (27)$$

$$Piling\left(\tfrac{ac}{day}\right) = \frac{Hrs/day}{Piling} \times Utilization \qquad (28)$$

Table 7—Summary of observed productivity for dozer processing residual slash (limbs and tops) and trees felled for in-woods piling and burning

	Slash from limbs and tops of merchantable trees (3-in top)	Whole trees, ≤3-in DBH
Maximum blade capacity (yd³)	5.78	5.78
Collection speed (ft/min)	57.20	57.20
Push to pile speed (ft/min)	57.20	57.20
Collect time (min/ac)	48.90	48.90
Slash volume (ft³/ac)	744.52	27.55
Number of blades/acre	19.08	0.71
Push time (min/ac)	50.04	1.85
In-woods piles (hrs/ac)	1.65	0.85
At landing piles (hrs/ac)	0.82	0.42

DBH = diameter at breast height.
Number of blades/acre = number of times the bulldozer pushed up slash on an acre basis.

Appendix 4. Labor Costs

The cost of labor to an employer includes basic wages, legally required benefits, and other fringe benefits. Basic wage rates are most often determined by the employer based on industry norms and local conditions, but wages are highly variable by region and tasks. A complete listing of average wage rates by state and industry type is published by the U.S. Department of Labor, Bureau of Labor Statistics (2007). For contracts involving federal dollars, employers may be required to pay wages at least equal to Davis-Bacon determinations (http://www.gpo.gov/davisbacon/).

Legally required benefits include social security tax, Medicare, state and federal unemployment insurance, and workers' compensation. The Social Security Act requires that businesses and employees pay a matching social security tax that provides for retirement, medical, and survivor benefits. Unemployment insurance, which differs by state, provides temporary and partial wage replacement to workers who have become unemployed through no fault of their own. Workers' compensation insurance covers most all types of private and public employment and rates are based on safety risk incidence by industry type and state (Dietz 1997).

Fringe benefits include voluntary employee benefits provided by employers in addition to legally required benefits. Fringe benefits may include group life and health insurance, vacation and holiday pay, sick leave, and retirement. Table 8 identifies rates used in the Harvest Cost-Revenue Estimator for legally required benefit rates (Ostwald 2002) and default fringe rates.

Table 8—Legally required benefit rates and default fringe rates used in the HCR Estimator

Employee benefits	Basic wage rate	HCR Estimator default rate
	Percent	
Legally required benefits paid by employer:		
Social security	6.20	6.20
Medicare	1.45	1.45
Federal unemployment	0.80	0.80
State unemployment	Varies by state	1.80
Workers' compensation	Varies by state and industry	36.00
Voluntary benefits paid by employer:		
Paid leave (holidays, vacation, sick leave)	Varies by employer	8.64
Insurance (life, health, disability)	Varies by employer	8.15
Retirement	Varies by employer	3.90

Appendix 5. Mobilization and Transportation Costs

Mobilization of equipment to the project site is calculated according to equations 29 and 30. Cost to mobilize each piece of equipment is a function of total time to transport, unloading, return for additional equipment, and loading equipment, which is also a function of transport speed and return empty speed. Mobilization cost per equipment piece is a function of mobilization time multiplied by labor costs per hour, and ownership and operating costs for both the semi-tractor and trailer used to move the equipment.

$$Mobilize\ (hr) = \left(\frac{Project\ Site\ (mi)}{Transport\ (mph)} + \frac{Project\ Site\ (mi)}{Empty\ Out\ (mph)} + load(hr) + unload(hr) \right) \qquad (29)$$

$$\frac{\$}{Equipment} = \qquad (30)$$

$$Mobilize\ (hr) \left(\frac{Labor\ \$}{hour} + \frac{Own\ and\ Operate\ Semi}{hour} + \frac{Own\ and\ Operate\ Trailer}{hour} \right)$$

Transportation costs of logs and chips are calculated according to equation 31. These costs are a function of average haul speed to the mill and backhaul speed to the project site, distance traveled between forest and mill, subcontracting cost per hour, time to hook up trailers in the woods, and time to drop a load of logs or chips at the mill or other wood products manufacturing/processing facility. Subcontracting cost per hour is a function of highway diesel fuel cost and driver wage rate. Total cost per truckload is multiplied by the total number of truckloads per project as calculated in appendix 1.

$$\frac{\$}{Load} = \frac{\$}{hr} \left(\frac{Mill\ (mi)}{Haul\ (mph)} + \frac{Mill\ (mi)}{Backhaul\ (mph)} + hook(hr) + drop(hr) \right) \qquad (31)$$

Alternatively, cost per load of logs or chips can be calculated as a function of price per mile as specified by the model user. Quoted per-mile costs are multiplied by the total number of miles driven to the mill and back to the project site. Here, cost per truckload incorporates allowable hook and drop times, average speed, highway diesel fuel cost, and driver wages.